CONTENTS

INTRODUCTION

There are plenty of diets out there that claim to help you lose weight, but at the end of the day, you lose little to no weight. With the Keto diet, you will not have to fuss with calories or containers. Counting calories or containers can be troublesome. With the Keto diet, all you need to remember is that the number of carbs you need to take in per day! You do not need to remember to write down the calorie count for each meal you eat or tally your containers. While doing these "counting diets," by the end of the day, you will eventually binge eat because you are not full. The food prescribed in this diet not only fuels you but keeps you full, too. All you need to do is follow the approved list of foods that this book will give you. The Keto diet works with your body's systems in order to maximize weight loss and introduce you to a new healthy and thinner you!

This book describes, in detail, what the Keto diet is and how it works. It will give you the tools to understand why the diet consists of certain foods and why eating or omitting these foods from your diet will be beneficial. This type of diet needs to be followed for a certain length of time in order it gain the maximum benefits it has to offer for weight loss. Following this plan may also help you with different ailments. Eating certain processed foods may cause your body's systems to react negatively, and your health may start to deteriorate. Being able to understand how this diet helps your body's system restore themselves back to their original state is pivotal. Restoring your body back to its natural state and getting back to a healthy weight will not be an easy accomplishment. Your body becomes dependent on processed foods that are toxic to you. When you remove the processed foods from your diet, it will cause your body to go into a surprising state, since you will only be eating natural and healthy foods. Your body will be eliminating all the toxins that it has been used to ingest. While your body is detoxing from the unhealthy starches, sugars, and other processed foods, you may experience what some people have dubbed the "Keto flu." This is short-term and has few side effects. Being able to cope with these side effects will help you get over the toughest part of the Keto diet which is not so tough! The book will help you implement the necessary steps you can do in order to try to prevent or minimize these short-lived side effects. You will also be given tools to help you stay motivated, so you are able to achieve the end results of weight loss. We all know it is not easy to start on a new diet. Especially a diet that makes your body come out of its comfort zone and goes through drastic changes to make you a healthier you. The tools and tips this book offers will help you stay focused and on track to a better you!

The Ketogenic Diet, What Is It?

Simply put, the ketogenic diet is a low-carb diet that is high in fat and includes a moderate amount of protein. After you follow the diet for a while, your body will go into a metabolic state which is known as ketosis. While in ketosis, your liver will switch from is a regular function and start to produce ketones. These ketones will move glucose out of the way and become your body's main source of energy.

So why is everyone going crazy about the diet? Well, for starters it will change how your body functions in the most natural way and change the way you view food as fuel.

And this is important since the keto diet is based on the premise that your body lags as a sugar burner and works better as a fat burner.

The Transition: From Sugar to Fat

Your body automatically produces glucose and insulin soon after you enjoy a yummy and yet carb pack treats like a sweet piece of cake or buttered bagel. Why does your body choose to produce glucose? It just so happens to be the easiest molecule for your body to convert and use as energy. It's also the main reason why your body prefers this energy source because it's so quick and easy. Now, your body produces insulin to process the glucose in your bloodstream as it goes through your body.

This sounds really efficient, right? It's fast and your body can get the energy it needs quickly so you can function. But the problem with this easy process is that your body can only use a limited amount of glucose as its main energy source. Anything else will be converted into fat and stored. And when your glucose levels start running low again, your body will also tell your brain you need to hurry up and grab a sugary or carb-filled snack to refill that energy source.

Now you see, this dangerous cycle of consuming unhealthy foods for energy can lead to excess body fat and of course health problems. The best way to stop this terrible cycle is to turn your body into a fat burner! And you can do this on the keto diet.

Once you lower your carb intake enough, your body will start to look for a different energy source – and this means ketosis is about to begin! When your body is in ketosis, it will produce ketones that only occur when the liver breaks down excess fat cells.

You're probably thinking why doesn't my body naturally do this if it's healthier for me? Well, when your body produces insulin, ketosis is essentially blocked because insulin prevents any fat cells from entering your bloodstream and from there they're just stored in your body.

But when you lower your carb intake, your glucose and blood sugar levels dramatically drop and in turn eventually lower your insulin levels. This opens a way for fat cells to finally release the water they're storing (aka water weight) and enter your bloodstream heading straight to your liver. Turning your useless fat cells into your go-to energy source is the main goal of the keto diet. Just remember, you won't get into ketosis by starving your body of food. You can only enter a state of ketosis by laying off the carbohydrates and sugar.

And don't worry; you won't miss those two when you start noticing all the physical and mental changes, which I'll get into next!

Benefits of the Ketogenic Diet

With so many different diets out there, you may be wondering why the ketogenic diet is one of the best options. This chapter outlines many of the reasons that you should begin the ketogenic diet. So, whether you want to lose weight or are looking to lower your risk for Type 2 diabetes, the ketogenic diet may be an excellent option for you. While the ketogenic diet can seem a bit overwhelming, especially considering all of the changes that it will have on how your body runs entirely, it is worth the extra effort given all of the incredible benefits that also come with it.

Weight Loss

Weight loss is the biggest reason that people begin any sort of diet in the first place, and high fat and low carb diets have been used for centuries for those who tend to carry a little extra weight. One of the greatest benefits of the ketogenic diet is that it suppresses your appetite. When you have a decreased appetite and lower insulin levels, your body's fat levels will also decrease. When you enter ketosis, you will also burn fat and use your fat storages as energy. It is a win-win for most people. On a regular diet, your body uses carbohydrates to create energy, and in return, your body stores the fat in unwanted places. On the ketogenic diet, this will not be an issue at all and you will begin to lose weight.

Lowered Blood Sugar Levels and Decreased Risk of Type 2 Diabetes

The ketogenic diet means that you will be lowering your insulin levels within your body. When this happens, you will begin to run off ketones and utilize the fat as fuel. One 2005 study published in Nutrition & Metabolism looked at the effectiveness of a low- carb ketogenic diet to treat type 2 diabetes. 28 overweight diabetic participants were recruited for the 16-week study, with 21 participants completing it. The researchers offered the participants counseling with a goal to limit their carb consumption to less than 20 grams per day while cutting back diabetes medication dosages. 7 of the participants were able to discontinue their diabetes medications while the mean body weight decreased by 6.6%. Their triglyceride levels also dropped by 42%.

Increase Lifespan

Some researchers found that some patients were able to lower the oxidative stress in their body when they were on the ketogenic diet. In return, this helped increase their lifespan by increasing their health. By lowering the insulin levels and using ketones as fuel, the oxidative stress was able to decrease.

PCOS (Polycystic Ovary Syndrome)

PCOS is a common side effect for women who are insulin resistant. Unfortunately, this can cause a number of hormonal issues such as infertility. Another 2005 study published in Nutrition & Metabolism, studied the effects of a low-carbohydrate, ketogenic diet on the polycystic ovary syndrome. Eleven women participated in the 24-week study who were told to limit their daily carb intake to no more than 20 grams/day. Five out of the eleven women completed the study, who showed noticeable improvements in their body weight (-12%), percent free testosterone levels (-22%), and fasting insulin (-54%). In fact, two of the women during this trial study became pregnant themselves!

Increased Brain Function

Increased brain function is another common reason that people choose to adopt the ketogenic diet. It is thought that this diet can help improve learning skills, memory recall, clarity of thought, and other cognitive functions. In studies done on humans, it was found that the ketogenic diet was beneficial to a person's brain function even over a short period. While on the ketogenic diet, it is possible to increase your ATP concentration and the number of hippocampal mitochondria in your brain by 50%. The hippocampus is the area of your brain that regulates our emotions, learning ability, and memory.

Mitochondrial Function

Many of our everyday functions such as immunity to common illnesses, sports performance, energy, and health are dependent on how the mitochondria in our body function. Mitochondria are the energy factories in our cells, so without them, we would not be able to function properly. Studies have found that these cells function much better while subjects are on a ketogenic diet. This is because the body is able to increase its energy levels in a more efficient, stable, and steady way while in ketosis. This is because mitochondria are specifically designed to use this fat for energy. When fat is used as the body's main source of energy, it's able to decrease any toxins, which increases energy output.

IBS (Irritable Bowel Syndrome)

If you suffer from IBS, the thought of being on a high-fat diet may seem like a bad idea, and, in fact, eating more fat will most likely end in bouts of diarrhea at first. Some studies have found that a diet that incorporates less sugar can provide relief to those who suffer from IBS and even improve stool habits, quality of life, and abdominal pain.

Energy

On a carb-loaded diet, you may experience what is known as a carb crash. This is because our bodies are not designed to run off excess amounts of sugars for long periods of time, hence why you often feel good after eating but are unable to sustain these energy levels throughout the day. When you switch to the ketogenic diet, you will experience higher, more stable energy levels throughout the day. On the ketogenic diet, you can finally say goodbye to afternoon slumps and caffeine cravings. When you switch your diet, you will have readily available fat as fuel, so you will be able to go hours without food and still maintain steady energy levels. If you are a person who is addicted to sugar and caffeine, the ketogenic diet may be the answer for you.

GERD (Gastroesophageal Reflux Disease)

There are many people who suffer from both heartburn and GERD. There was a study done by the Journal of Digestive Disease and Science which found that individuals who were on the ketogenic diet, even if it was for less than a week, we're able to lower the acidity in their esophagus. These people reported that their heartburn conditions were less severe while on the ketogenic diet. These reductions were most likely linked to upping their fat and lowering the amount of carbohydrates in their diet.

Headaches and Migraines

For some, switching to the ketogenic diet also helps to decrease the number of migraines they experience. Additionally, it was found that the ketogenic diet helped to reduce the number of drugs people used to help with their headache and migraine symptoms.

Stabilized Moods

The ketogenic diet has also been used to help patients who have autism. More research needs to be done, but there is a potential link between the ketogenic diet and being effective for autism. In a research paper following the use of the ketogenic diet with patients on the autism spectrum, studies found that there were many benefits to mood stabilization. In one specific study, children with autism showed milder autistic behaviors when placed on a diet with 30% MCT oil for six months. Other reports showed that the ketogenic diet can also help with mood stabilization for people who suffer from bipolar disorder.

Epilepsy

As previously mentioned in chapter one, the ketogenic diet was originally designed to help patients with epilepsy. In the modern world of research, there are more beneficial ways to help with epilepsy, though some studies found that the ketogenic diet can still be helpful with the treatment.

Increased Self Control

Later in this book, we will discuss fasting in order to get into the ketosis state. For many people, the thought of going twelve or more hours without food seems like absolute torture, but once you adapt to using fat as energy, fasting and self-control will become much easier.

Alzheimer's

People who have Alzheimer's suffer from a condition where their brain is unable to use glucose. As a result, this often leads to high levels of inflammation, and some scientists even refer to this as "type 3" diabetes. Thus, the ketogenic diet is incredibly beneficial if the brain is unable to use glucose. By using ketones, this may assist those who have Alzheimer's.

Cancer

Cancer is another reason people adopt the ketogenic diet and why it continues to gain popularity. Scientists believe that cancer cells are able to thrive on glucose as their main fuel resource. On the ketogenic diet, this source of glucose is taken away and deprives the cancer cells of the energy it needs to thrive. In one 2012 study, ten patients were put on a ketogenic diet and after 28 days, one patient experienced partial remission, five were able to stabilize, and four showed continued progress.

Acne

If you suffer from acne, the ketogenic diet may be beneficial for you. This is because studies have shown that foods high in glycemic are one of the reasons that acne outbreaks are stimulated, so when you are eating foods that are lower in glycemic on the ketogenic diet, you reduce your chances of developing acne.

Digestive Health Booster

While on the ketogenic diet, you will increase the level of fiber in your diet via (mostly) non-starchy vegetables and healthy fruits. By increasing the amount of fiber in your diet, you can improve your digestive health. In addition, you will also be able to lower your risk of gastric ulcers, colorectal cancer, cramping, bloating, diarrhea, and constipation.

Decreased Blood Pressure

Another benefit of the ketogenic diet is increased levels of potassium and lower levels of sugars. While this is a major benefit for weight loss, it's also beneficial for those who suffer from high blood pressure.

Endurance Performance

Studies have found that the ketogenic diet is beneficial in helping athletes increase their overall performance. This can be due to the lower lactate load in the body, as well as lowered oxidative stress when the body is fueled by fat. Other studies have found that higher levels of ketones in the blood lead to increased energy over a thirty-minute period.

Overall Health Benefits

As with any diet, the ketogenic diet can offer general health benefits within your everyday life. It can help to improve your cholesterol levels, reduce your fat and weight, and decrease your triglyceride levels. Overall, the diet offers a lot of health benefits.

As you can see, there are many incredible benefits to the ketogenic diet which can help you to change your life. Of course, as with any diet, there are certain downfalls that may be holding you back from starting the diet in the first place. If you are hesitant in your decision about whether if the ketogenic diet is best for you, refer to the third chapter to read about the adverse effects of the ketogenic diet.

Before you begin the ketogenic diet, it's important that you go over the diet with a medical professional such as your family doctor. The ketogenic diet can be a big change that may be too much for everyone. So, while there are many benefits to this diet, it's important to follow the ketogenic diet in a way that is healthy.

If you are ready to continue, continue onto the fourth chapter which covers the beginnings of the ketogenic diet plan where you will be given a list of foods to consume, foods to avoid, and a basic meal plan to follow. Pretty soon, you will be well on your way to starting (and sticking with) the ketogenic diet.

What You Can Eat And What You Should Avoid

For being a restrictive diet, the list of foods you can eat is relatively extensive. All kinds of meat and seafood (ideally grass-fed, wild-caught, and organic) are allowed, while all full-fat dairy is also encouraged. You can eat lots of low-carb vegetables, as well, though you're more limited on fruit. A banana every now and then shouldn't throw you out of ketosis, however, but you should always be careful about what else you eat that day. Here's a fairly complete list of everything

Food to Eat

Meat/seafood:
- Beef (ideally grass-fed)
- Eggs (ideally cage-free and organic)

- Fish/shellfish (ideally wild-caught)
- Goat
- Lamb
- Organ meats
- Pork (ideally free-range and organic)
- Poultry (organic)

Vegetables/fruit:

- Alfalfa sprouts
- Avocado
- Berries (blackberries, raspberries, cranberries, etc)
- Bell peppers
- Bok choy
- Broccoli
- Button mushrooms
- Cabbage
- Cauliflower
- Celery
- Citrus (lemons, oranges, limes)
- Cucumber
- Eggplant
- Garlic
- Kale
- Lettuce
- Onions
- Parsley
- Radishes
- Sea vegetables
- Spinach
- Swiss chard
- Tomatoes
- Watercress
- Zucchini

Nuts/seeds (in moderation):

- Almonds
- Brazil nuts
- Chia seeds
- Flax seeds
- Macadamia nuts

- Pecans
- Pumpkin seeds
- Shredded coconut (unsweetened)
- Sunflower seeds
- Walnuts

Full-fat dairy:
- Cheese (cheddar, parmesan, mozzarella, brie, ricotta, etc)
- Cottage cheese
- Cream cheese
- Dairy-free milk alternatives (unsweetened almond milk, coconut milk, macadamia nut milk)
- Greek yogurt (plain and unsweetened)
- Heavy cream

Fats/oils:
- Almond oil
- Avocado oil
- Cocoa butter
- Coconut oil/coconut cream
- Duck fat
- Ghee (clarified butter)
- Nut butters (in moderation)
- Olive oil (cold-pressed extra-virgin)

Beverages:
- Sparkling water + seltzers (w/out added sweeteners)
- Unsweetened coconut water
- Unsweetened coffee (or sweetened with natural o-calorie sweetener)
- Unsweetened herbal tea (or sweetened with natural o-calorie sweetener)
- Water

Baking/cooking supplies:
- Almond flour
- Baking powder/baking soda (aluminum-free)
- Coconut aminos (soy sauce substitute)
- Coconut flour
- Erythritol/stevia blends
- Fish sauce
- Mayonnaise (w/out added sugar)
- Monk fruit extract or powder
- Psyllium husk (a thickener)

- Spices + herbs
- Sugar-free ketchup
- Sugar-free yellow mustard
- Vinegar (white, wine, and apple cider)
- Xanthan gum (in very small amounts)

Foods to avoid

Knowing what to avoid on the ketogenic diet is determined by asking yourself two questions: Is it low-carb? Does it have artificial ingredients? Foods too high in carbs will throw you out of ketosis when you eat too much, while anything with artificial or processed ingredients also tends to be too high in carbs, while also being just unhealthy. Here's what to avoid:

Processed meats:

- Deli meat
- Grain-fed meats
- Hot dogs
- Sausages

Grain:

- Barley
- Buckwheat
- Corn
- Oatmeal
- Quinoa
- Rice
- Wheat
- Wheat gluten

High-carb veggies and fruit:

- Artichokes
- Bananas
- Carrots
- Clementines
- Dried fruit
- Fruit syrups
- Grapes
- Jam/jelly
- Kiwi
- Mangos
- Pears
- Pineapple

- Potatoes
- Squash
- Sweet potatoes
- Watermelon
- Yams

Low-fat or fat-free dairy:
- Fake butter alternatives
- Low-fat/fat-free cream cheese
- Low-fat/fat-free sour cream
- Low-fat/fat-free yogurt
- Skim milk

Beans/legumes:
- Black
- Chickpeas
- Fava
- Kidney
- Lentils
- Peas
- White

Certain oils:
- Canola
- Corn
- Grapeseed
- Peanut
- Sesame
- Soybean
- Sunflower

Refined + artificial sweeteners:
- Agave
- Aspartame
- Cane sugar
- Coconut sugar
- Corn syrup
- Equal
- Honey
- Maple syrup
- Raw sugar
- Saccharin

- Splenda
- Sucralose
- White sugar

Other:

- Alcohol
- Baked goods + treats
- Diet foods
- Fast food

The Most Common Mistakes People Make On The Keto Diet

The ketogenic diet isn't the easiest to follow. You have to be careful to eliminate certain foods and ingredients like wheat and sugar, which like to hide in sometimes surprising foods, and you have to stick to your percentages of fat, protein, and carbs. People don't even think about certain things when they start out, which can make the diet harder or not as beneficial. Here are the most common mistakes to avoid (and what to do instead):

Mistake #1: Not planning ahead

You decide to go on the ketogenic diet and dive right in. Unfortunately, you still have a kitchen full of foods not allowed on the keto diet and no idea what to make for meals. You also don't know what restaurants have keto-friendly options or what brands you should look for at the store. This makes your new diet very difficult, and you always feel at a loss and tempted to break the diet. As soon as you make the decision to go keto, get rid of everything in your house that isn't keto-approved. Look up recipes and start meal-planning, so you know exactly what to get at the store. You'll feel much more prepared and less overwhelmed.

Mistake #2: Not anticipating the keto flu

The keto flu is what happens when your body transitions from burning carbs to burning fat. Symptoms include headaches, fatigue, and nausea. While most people get through it without too much trouble in a week or two, it can be uncomfortable, especially if you aren't prepared for it. If you go about your normal routine and don't know what to do when symptoms hit, you may start regretting your choice to go keto and back out. You'll feel discouraged and disappointed in yourself. If you accept that the keto flu is coming, however, you can do things to make it easier. Staying hydrated is very important, since you lose more water during this phase of the diet. You should also eat as much protein and fats as you need, without worrying about the percentages, and be sure to replenish your electrolytes (especially sodium) by drinking chicken broth with salt. If your symptoms are especially bad, it's okay to eat some clean carbs (like a sweet potato or high-carb fruit) to make the adjustment easier.

Mistake #3: Not adjusting your exercise routine

Some people worry that they can't build muscle on the keto diet, but you definitely can. You just have to adjust your routines and possibly the diet slightly to make the most of your workouts. Anaerobic exercise, which is intense and interval-based, isn't improved by the keto diet because it relies on carbs. You can still do this type of exercise, but you should eat 15-30 fast-acting carbs before and after a workout. Aerobic and cardio exercise, however, can improve with the keto diet and doesn't require any adjustments to your carb intake.

Mistake #4: Ignoring your electrolytes

Electrolytes are necessary to good health. On the keto diet, you lose them more than on other diets, especially during the first weeks of ketosis. Many people neglect these minerals, which can lead to potentially serious health problems. Be sure to get sodium, magnesium, potassium, and calcium through food or supplements, if necessary. Talk to your doctor about testing your levels, and be aware of how much you need per day for your best health.

Mistake #5: Not getting good sleep

Sleep is just as important to the body and mind as good food. Without good sleep, your health will suffer. A lot of people have terrible sleep habits, like getting distracted by their phone and computers in bed, never getting up at the same time, and so on. There's a lot you can do to improve your sleep quality. Make sure the room is completely dark and free from electronic blue lights, which have been shown to disrupt good sleep patterns. Start winding down an half or half-hour before bed, and turn off the TV and keep away from your phone and computer. Give your mind the chance to settle and prepare the body for sleep.

Mistake #6: Not finding support

When you change your diet dramatically, it will be hard. Lots of people believe they can do it alone, but they're soon overwhelmed and discouraged. It's very difficult to do anything by yourself; humans are built for community. To ensure long-term success, find a good support network, whether it's people who are going keto themselves, or are just really good listeners and cheerleaders. Consider looking online for a group on a website like MeetUp. You should also be clear with your family (if they aren't going keto with you) about what you need from them in terms of support. That might mean asking that they keep treats out of the house or that they agree to eating only keto meals if you're cooking. With good support, you'll find the motivation you need to stick to your diet.

Keto Diet FAQs

How much time does it take for me to get into ketosis?

The thing you need to understand here first is that a Ketogenic diet is not some typical diet you can do just when you want it. Getting into ketosis takes time and you must have patience, it usually takes about 2 to 7 days before your body can adapt to the new diet, this depends still on the size of your body, your activity levels, and the foods you are eating.

A way to easily get into ketosis is to try exercising with an empty stomach then reduce your carb intake to 20 g or less each day, and lastly, drink a lot of water.

Where can I find low carb foods or recipes?

Easiest way? Probably the internet, you can search about the foods needed to eat when in a Ketogenic diet, and some of those sites will provide recipes on certain foods. Believe it or not but there are also high carb foods you can convert into low carbs, isn't that great? Pretty convenient, you just need to find and follow the correct recipe then you are good to go.

Is there a way to help me track my carb intake?

Yes! There are certain mobile apps you can download that can help you track your carb intake.

Is too much fat good on this diet?

YES! It is the main reason why you are doing this type of diet, it focuses on fats rather than carbs. This will help you make your body use fats as energy, and in this way, it can help you lose weight quickly. But you know if it is "more than too much" and that is just bad. There are certain guides on the internet you can follow in order for you to execute this diet correctly.

Can I know how much weight will I lose?

In this time, it is upon you. It depends on you on how much weight you want to lose. Because it is the main goal of this diet, for you to lose weight, so eventually you are going to lose it, but you can speed up the process and lose more if you are going to add exercises than your normal one, increase the time you execute those exercises, cutting off some foods not needed in the diet, and many more. There are many ways on how you can do this and finish the diet with your desired outcome.

How does ketosis function?

To sum it all up, ketosis is a state where our body adapts into eating fats rather than carbohydrates, in this way, the body will use the eaten fats and the body fats itself as the primary source of energy we use in daily activities. At some point, it is not just healthy for the body but also for the mind.

So you may ask, where does the energy from fats come from?

To answer this, when our body enters the state of "Ketosis" our body lets our liver to break down those fats into molecules called ketones, and these ketones are the ones who give us the energy.

Another question is, how does it help in losing weight?

Well, lack in calories due to this diet makes our body use its own fats in order to produce and use the energy we once get from the foods we eat, thus making it a great way to lose weight.

Now you know, how ketogenic diet works it is up to you if you will implement the diet. Just weigh in the options and be yourself. One advice that I can give you is do not eliminate the virtue of hard work when it comes to losing weight because it is crucial in making a certain diet or routine successful. Always give it a try and see if it will work well for you but before we part ways I would like to congratulate you because you are on your way to a fitter and healthier you! Wishing you all the best!

KETO DIET BREAKFAST RECIPES FOR TWO

Quick Raspberry Vanilla Shake:

Serves: 2
Preparation Time: 7 minutes
Nutritional information per serving:
Calories: 213
Fat: 13.4 g
Net Carbs: 7.7 g
Protein: 4.5 g
Ingredients:

- 2 cups raspberries
- 2 tablespoons erythritol
- 6 raspberries to garnish
- ½ cups cold unsweetened almond milk
- 2/3 teaspoons vanilla extract
- ½ cups heavy whipping cream

Instructions for Cooking:

1. In a large blender, process the raspberries, milk, vanilla extract, whipping cream, and erythritol for 2 minutes; work in two batches if needed. The shake should be frosty.
2. Pour into glasses, stick in straws, garnish with raspberries and serve.

Bacon & Cream Cheese Mug Muffins:

Serves: 2

Preparation Time: 10 minutes

<u>Nutritional information per serving:</u>

Calories: 511

Fat: 38 g

Net Carbs: 4.5 g

Protein: 16 g

<u>Ingredients:</u>

- ¼ cup flax meal
- 1 egg
- 2 tablespoons heavy cream
- 2 tablespoons pesto
- ¼ cup almond flour
- ¼ teaspoon baking soda
- Salt and black pepper to taste
- 2 tablespoons cream cheese
- 4 slices bacon
- ½ medium avocado, sliced

<u>Instructions for Cooking:</u>

1. Mix together flax meal, flour, and baking soda in a bowl.
2. Add egg, heavy cream, and pesto, and whisk well. Season with salt and pepper.
3. Divide the mixture between 2 ramekins. Microwave for 60-90 seconds.
4. Let cool slightly before filling. In a nonstick skillet, cook bacon until crispy; set aside.
5. Invert the muffins onto a plate and cut in half, crosswise.
6. Assemble the sandwiches by spreading cream cheese and topping with bacon and avocado slices.

Keto Smoked Salmon, Avocado and Egg Butter:

Serves: 2

Preparation Time: 10 minutes

<u>Nutritional information per serving:</u>

Calories: 1278

Fat: 116 g

Net Carbs: 5 g

Protein: 50 g

<u>Ingredients:</u>

- 4 eggs
- 2 avocados
- 5 ounces of softened butter
- 4 ounces smoked salmon
- Salt
- Pepper
- 2 tablespoons extra-virgin olive oil
- 1 tablespoon fresh parsley

<u>Instructions for Cooking:</u>

1. Place the eggs in a pot of cold water and bring to a boil over medium heat.
2. Once boiling, lower the heat setting and simmer for 8 minutes.
3. Remove the eggs from the pot and place them in cold water to cool them. Peel the eggs and finely chop them.
4. Now mix the eggs and butter together with a fork. Add salt and pepper as desired.
5. Serve the egg butter combination with several slices of smoked salmon and an avocado, diced and tossed in olive oil. Garnish with parsley.

Classic Eggs with Canadian Bacon:

Serves: 2

Preparation Time: 15 minutes

<u>Nutritional information per serving:</u>

Calories: 326

Fat: 13.3 g

Net Carbs: 5.2 g

Protein: 46 g

<u>Ingredients:</u>

- 2 (1-ounce) slices Canadian bacon
- 4 eggs
- 1/4 teaspoon ground black pepper
- Salt, to season
- 8 cherry tomatoes, halves

<u>Instructions for Cooking:</u>

1. Heat up a nonstick aluminum pan over a medium-high flame. Once hot, fry the bacon until crispy; reserve, living the rendered fat in the pan.
2. Turn the heat to medium-low. Crack the eggs into the bacon grease. Cover the pan with a lid and fry the eggs until they are cooked through.
3. Salt and pepper to taste.
4. Serve with the reserved bacon and cherry tomatoes on the side. Enjoy!

Golden Turmeric Latte with Nutmeg:

Serves: 2

Preparation Time: 7 minutes

Nutritional information per serving:

Calories: 153

Fat: 13.2 g

Net Carbs: 0.9 g

Protein: 3.9 g

Ingredients:

- 2 cups almond milk
- 1/3 teaspoons cinnamon powder
- ½ cup brewed coffee
- ¼ teaspoon turmeric powder
- 1 teaspoon xylitol
- Nutmeg powder to garnish

Instructions for Cooking:

1. Add the almond milk, cinnamon powder, coffee, turmeric, and xylitol in the blender.
2. Blend the ingredients at medium speed for 50 seconds and pour the mixture into a saucepan.
3. Over low heat, set the pan and heat through for 6 minutes, without boiling.
4. Keep swirling the pan to prevent from boiling. Turn the heat off, and serve in latte cups, topped with nutmeg powder.

Italian Omelet:

Serves: 2
Preparation Time: 15 minutes
<u>Nutritional information per serving</u>:
Calories: 451
Fat: 36.5 g
Net Carbs: 3 g
Protein: 30 g
<u>Ingredients:</u>

- 4 eggs
- 4 oz. mozzarella, grated
- 2 tablespoons butter
- 8 thin slices chorizo
- 1 tomato, sliced
- Salt and black pepper to taste

<u>Instructions for Cooking:</u>

1. Whisk the eggs with salt and pepper. Melt butter in a skillet and cook the eggs for 30 seconds.
2. Spread the chorizo slices over. Arrange the sliced tomato and mozzarella over the chorizo.
3. Cook for about 3 minutes. Cover the skillet and continue cooking for 3 more minutes until omelet is completely set.
4. Run a spatula around the edges of the omelet and flip it onto a plate, folded side down. Serve.

Paprika Omelet with Goat Cheese:

Serves: 2

Preparation Time: 10 minutes

Nutritional information per serving:

Calories: 287

Fat: 22.6 g

Net Carbs: 1.3 g

Protein: 19.8 g

Ingredients:

- 2 teaspoons ghee, room temperature
- 4 eggs, whisked
- 4 tablespoons goat cheese
- 1 teaspoon paprika
- Sea salt and ground black pepper, to taste

Instructions for Cooking:

1. Melt the ghee in a pan over medium heat.
2. Add the whisked eggs to the pan and cover with the lid; reduce the heat to medium-low.
3. Cook for 4 minutes; now, stir in the cheese and paprika; continue to cook an additional 3 minutes or until cheese has melted.
4. Season with salt
5. And pepper and serve immediately. Enjoy!

Coconut Shake with Avocado:

Serves: 2
Preparation Time: 4 minutes
<u>Nutritional information per serving:</u>
Calories: 395
Fat: 27 g
Net Carbs: 3.4 g
Protein: 13.7 g
<u>Ingredients:</u>

- 3 cups coconut milk, chilled
- 1 avocado, pitted, peeled, sliced
- 2 tablespoons erythritol
- Coconut cream for topping

<u>Instructions for Cooking:</u>

1. Combine the coconut milk, avocado, and erythritol, into the smoothie maker, and blend for 1 minute to smooth.
2. Pour the drink into serving glasses, lightly add some coconut cream on top of them, and garnish with mint leaves. Serve immediately.

Herbed Buttered Eggs:

Serves: 2

Preparation Time: 15 minutes

Nutritional information per serving:

Calories: 321

Fat: 21 g

Net Carbs: 2.5 g

Protein: 12 g

Ingredients:

- 1 tablespoon coconut oil
- 2 tablespoons butter
- 1 teaspoon fresh thyme
- 4 eggs
- 2 garlic cloves, minced
- ½ cup chopped parsley
- ½ cup chopped cilantro
- ¼ teaspoon cumin
- ¼ teaspoon cayenne pepper
- Salt and black pepper to taste

Instructions for Cooking:

1. Warm coconut oil and butter in a skillet and add garlic and thyme; cook for 30 seconds.
2. Sprinkle with parsley and cilantro. Carefully crack the eggs into the skillet.
3. Lower the heat and cook for 4-6 minutes.
4. Adjust the seasoning. When the eggs are set, turn the heat off and serve.

Omelet with Vegetables and Mexican Cotija Cheese:

Serves: 2

Preparation Time: 15 minutes

<u>Nutritional information per serving:</u>

Calories: 287

Fat: 20.5 g

Net Carbs: 7.2 g

Protein: 17.4 g

<u>Ingredients:</u>

- 2 teaspoons olive oil
- 2 scallion stalks, chopped
- 2 garlic cloves, minced
- 2 bell peppers, chopped
- 1/2 cup cauliflower florets
- 3 eggs
- 1/2 teaspoon cayenne pepper
- Kosher salt and ground black pepper, to season
- 1/2 teaspoon dried Mexican oregano
- 1/2 teaspoon chili pepper flakes
- 1/2 teaspoon dried parsley flakes
- 2 ounces Cotija cheese, crumbled

<u>Instructions for Cooking:</u>

1. Heat the olive oil in a medium-sized pan over moderate heat.
2. Sauté the scallions and garlic until just tender and fragrant.
3. Now, stir in the peppers and cauliflower and continue sautéing an additional 2 to 3 minutes.
4. Meanwhile, mix the eggs with the cayenne pepper, salt, black pepper, oregano, chili pepper flakes, and parsley.
5. Pour the egg mixture over the sautéed vegetables. Let it cook, tilting your pan so the raw parts can cook.
6. Add the Cotija cheese, fold over and leave for 1 minute before slicing and serving. Enjoy!

Omelet Wrap with Avocado and Salmon:

Serves: 2
Preparation Time: 15 minutes
Nutritional information per serving:
Calories: 514
Fat: 47 g
Net Carbs: 5.8 g
Protein: 37 g
Ingredients:
- 1 avocado, sliced
- 2 tablespoons chopped chives
- 2 oz. smoked salmon, sliced
- 1 spring onion, sliced
- 4 eggs, beaten
- 3 tablespoons cream cheese
- 2 tablespoons butter
- Salt and black pepper to taste

Instructions for Cooking:
1. In a small bowl, combine the chives and cream cheese; set aside.
2. Season the eggs with salt and pepper. Melt butter in a pan and add the eggs; cook for 3 minutes.
3. Flip the omelet over and cook for another 2 minutes until golden.
4. Remove to a plate and spread the chive mixture over.
5. Top with salmon, avocado, and onion slices. Wrap and serve.

Spicy Masala and Brown Mushroom Omelet:

Serves: 2

Preparation Time: 15 minutes

<u>Nutritional information per serving:</u>

Calories: 217

Fat: 15.6 g

Net Carbs: 5 g

Protein: 14.4 g

<u>Ingredients:</u>

- 1 tablespoon olive oil
- 1/2 brown onion, thinly sliced
- 1 garlic clove, thinly sliced
- 1 green chili, minced
- 1/2 pound brown mushrooms, sliced
- 4 eggs, whisked
- 1 tablespoon fresh coriander, chopped
- Sea salt and ground black pepper, to taste
- 1/2 teaspoon Kashmiri chili powder
- 1/2 teaspoon garam masala

<u>Instructions for Cooking:</u>

1. In a nonstick skillet, heat the olive oil until sizzling.
2. Then, sauté the onion until translucent.
3. Now, stir in the garlic, chili pepper, and mushrooms and continue sautéing until just tender and fragrant or about 2 minutes. Reserve.
4. Add in the whisked eggs, fresh coriander, salt, black pepper, Kashmiri chili powder, and garam masala. Give it a quick swirl to distribute the eggs evenly across the skillet. Cook for 2 to 3 minutes.
5. Flip your omelet over and cook an additional minute or so.
6. Fill with the mushroom mixture, fold and serve immediately. Bon appétit!

KETO DIET POULTRY RECIPES FOR TWO

Cheese and Bacon Stuffed Chicken:

Serves: 2
Preparation Time: 30 minutes
Nutritional information per serving:
Calories: 401
Fat: 23.9 g
Net Carbs: 3.7 g
Protein: 41.2 g

Ingredients:

- 2 chicken fillets, skinless and boneless
- 1/2 teaspoon oregano
- 1/2 teaspoon tarragon
- 1/2 teaspoon paprika
- 1/4 teaspoon ground black pepper
- Sea salt, to taste
- 2 (1-ounce) slices bacon
- 2 (1-ounce) slices cheddar cheese
- 1 tomato, sliced

Instructions for Cooking:

1. Sprinkle the chicken fillets with oregano, tarragon, paprika, black pepper, and salt.
2. Place the bacon slices and cheese on each chicken fillet. Roll up the fillets and secure with toothpicks.
3. Place the stuffed chicken fillets on a lightly greased baking pan. Scatter the sliced tomato around the fillets.
4. Bake in the preheated oven at 390° F for 15 minutes; turn on the other side and bake an additional 5 to 10 minutes or until the meat is no longer pink.
5. Discard the toothpicks and serve immediately. Bon appétit!

Duck & Vegetable Casserole:

Serves: 2

Preparation Time: 20 minutes

<u>Nutritional information per serving:</u>

Calories: 433

Fat: 21 g

Net Carbs: 8 g

Protein: 53 g

<u>Ingredients:</u>

- 2 duck breasts, skin on and sliced
- 2 zucchinis, sliced
- 1 tablespoon coconut oil
- 1 green onion bunch, chopped
- 1 carrot, chopped
- 2 green bell peppers, seeded and chopped
- Salt and ground black pepper, to taste

<u>Instructions for Cooking:</u>

1. Set a pan over medium-high heat and warm oil, stir in the green onions, and cook for 2 minutes.
2. Place in the zucchini, bell peppers, pepper, salt, and carrot, and cook for 10 minutes.
3. Set another pan over medium-high heat, add in duck slices and cook each side for 3 minutes.
4. Pour the mixture into the vegetable pan. Cook for 3 minutes. Set in bowls and enjoy.

Dijon Chicken Breasts with Brussel Sprouts:

Serves: 2

Preparation Time: 15 minutes

<u>Nutritional information per serving:</u>

Calories: 580

Fat: 35.5 g

Net Carbs: 6.9 g

Protein: 52 g

<u>Ingredients:</u>

- 2 chicken breasts
- 1 cup Brussel sprouts, trimmed and halved
- 1/3 teaspoon salt
- 1/3 teaspoon pepper
- 2 tablespoons olive oil
- 1/3 cup balsamic vinegar

<u>For the marinade</u>

- 1/3 cup soy sauce
- 1/3 cup olive oil
- 2 teaspoons paprika
- 1 ½ teaspoons pepper
- 1 teaspoon salt
- 1 ½ tablespoon Dijon mustard
- 2 tablespoons fresh parsley, finely chopped

<u>Instructions for Cooking:</u>

1. In a large bowl whisk the soy sauce, olive oil, paprika, pepper, salt, Dijon mustard, and fresh parsley to make the marinade.
2. Add the chicken breasts in a large zip-top bag and pour in the marinade. Place in your refrigerator for 30 minutes.
3. Place the Brussel sprouts in a large baking dish lined with parchment paper.
4. Then add the marinated chicken breasts to the baking dish with Brussel sprouts. Sprinkle with salt, pepper and olive oil.
5. Bake for 15 minutes in a preheated oven to 420°F. Serve immediately and drizzle with balsamic vinegar. Enjoy!

Paleo Coconut Flour Chicken Nuggets:

Serves: 2

Preparation Time: 30 minutes

<u>Nutritional information per serving:</u>

Calories: 417

Fat: 37 g

Net Carbs: 4.3 g

Protein: 35 g

<u>Ingredients:</u>

- ½ cup coconut flour
- 1 egg
- 2 tablespoons garlic powder
- 2 chicken breasts, cubed
- Salt and black pepper, to taste
- ½ cup butter

<u>Instructions for Cooking:</u>

1. In a bowl, combine salt, garlic powder, flour, and pepper, and stir.
2. In a separate bowl, beat the egg.
3. Add the chicken in egg mixture, then in the flour mixture. Set a pan over medium heat and warm butter.
4. Add in chicken nuggets, and cook for 6 minutes on each side.
5. Remove to paper towels, drain the excess grease and serve.

Bacon-Wrapped Turkey Breast:

Serves: 2

Preparation Time: 1 hour 10 minutes

<u>Nutritional information per serving:</u>

Calories: 162

Fat: 3.1 g

Net Carbs: 0.8 g

Protein: 11.3 g

<u>Ingredients:</u>

- ¾ pound turkey breast
- ½ teaspoon dried thyme
- ½ teaspoon dried rosemary
- ½ teaspoon dried, ground sage
- Salt and ground black pepper, as required
- 6 large bacon slices

<u>Instructions for Cooking:</u>

1. Preheat the oven to 350₀ F. Line a baking sheet with parchment paper.
2. Sprinkle the turkey breast with herb mixture, salt and black pepper.
3. Arrange the bacon slices onto a smooth surface in a row with the slices, pressing against each other.
4. Place turkey breast on top of the bacon slices.
5. Wrap the end pieces of bacon around the turkey breast first, followed by the middle pieces.
6. Arrange wrapped turkey breast onto the prepared baking sheet.
7. With a piece of foil, cover the turkey breast loosely and bake for about 50 minutes.
8. Remove the foil and bake for about 10 more minutes.
9. Remove from the oven and place the turkey breast onto a platter for about 5-10 minutes before slicing.
10. With a sharp knife, cut the turkey breast into desired size slices and serve.

Traditional Turkish Chicken Kebabs:

Serves: 2
Preparation Time: 20 minutes
<u>Nutritional information per serving:</u>
Calories: 498
Fat: 23.2 g
Net Carbs: 6.2 g
Protein: 61 g
<u>Ingredients:</u>

- 1 pound chicken thighs, boneless, skinless and halved
- 1/2 cup Greek-style yogurt
- Sea salt, to taste
- 1 tablespoon Aleppo red pepper flakes
- 1/2 teaspoon ground black pepper
- 1/4 teaspoon dried oregano
- 1/2 teaspoon mustard seeds
- 1/8 teaspoon ground cinnamon
- 1/2 teaspoon sumac
- 2 Roma tomatoes, chopped
- 2 tablespoons olive oil
- 1 ½ ounce Swiss cheese, sliced

<u>Instructions for Cooking:</u>

1. Place the chicken thighs, yogurt, salt, red pepper flakes, black pepper, oregano, mustard seeds, cinnamon, sumac, tomatoes, and olive oil in a ceramic dish.
2. Cover and let it marinate in your refrigerator for 4 hours.
3. Preheat your grill for medium-high heat and lightly oil the grate.
4. Thread the chicken thighs onto skewers, making a thick log shape.
5. Cook your kebabs for 3 or 4 minutes; turn over and continue cooking for 3 to 4 minutes more.
6. An instant-read thermometer should read about 165₀ F.
7. Add the cheese and let it cook for a further 3 to 4 minutes or until completely melted. Bon appétit!

Chicken with Anchovy Tapenade:

Serves: 2
Preparation Time: 30 minutes
Nutritional information per serving:
Calories: 155
Fat: 13 g
Net Carbs: 3 g
Protein: 25 g
Ingredients:
- 1 chicken breast, cut into 4 pieces
- 2 tablespoons coconut oil
- 3 garlic cloves, and crushed

For the tapenade
- 1 cup black olives, pitted
- 1 oz. anchovy fillets, rinsed
- 1 garlic clove, crushed
- Salt and ground black pepper, to taste
- 2 tablespoons olive oil
- ¼ cup fresh basil, chopped
- 1 tablespoon lemon juice

Instructions for Cooking:
1. Using a food processor, combine the olives, salt, olive oil, basil, lemon juice, anchovy fillets, and pepper, blend well.
2. Set a pan over medium-high heat and warm coconut oil, stir in the garlic, and cook for 2 minutes.
3. Place in the chicken pieces and cook each side for 4 minutes.
4. Split the chicken among plates and apply a topping of the anchovy tapenade.

Creamy Chicken with Fresh Asparagus:

Serves: 2
Preparation Time: 15 minutes
Nutritional information per serving:
Calories: 506
Fat: 38 g
Net Carbs: 6.8 g
Protein: 46 g
Ingredients:

- 2 medium chicken breasts
- Salt and pepper, to taste
- 2 tablespoons olive oil
- 1 lb. fresh asparagus, trimmed and cut into 2-inch pieces
- 2 cloves garlic, sliced
- 2 teaspoons lemon juice
- 2 tablespoons butter
- ½ cup parmesan cheese, grated

Instructions for Cooking:

1. Heat the olive oil in a medium pan. Season the chicken breasts with salt and pepper.
2. Fry the chicken breasts for 4-5 minutes per side or until golden brown and set aside.
3. In a medium skillet place the butter and the minced garlic. Cook for 30 seconds.
4. Then add the fresh asparagus. Cook for 2-3 minutes or until the asparagus get tender.
5. Season with salt and pepper. Drizzle with the lemon juice and set aside.
6. Serve the chicken breasts and garnish with the asparagus and grated parmesan cheese.

Greek-Style Chicken Mélange:

Serves: 2
Preparation Time: 35 minutes
Nutritional information per serving:
Calories: 352
Fat: 14.3 g
Net Carbs: 5.9 g
Protein: 44.2 g
Ingredients:

- 2 ounces bacon, diced
- 3/4 pound whole chicken, boneless and chopped
- 1/2 medium-sized leek, chopped
- 1 teaspoon ginger garlic paste
- 1 teaspoon poultry seasoning mix
- Sea salt, to taste
- 1 bay leaf
- 1 thyme sprig
- 1 rosemary sprig
- 1 cup chicken broth
- 1/2 cup cauliflower, chopped into small florets
- 2 vine-ripe tomatoes, pureed

Instructions for Cooking:

1. Heat a medium-sized pan over medium-high heat; once hot, fry the bacon until it is crisp or about 3 minutes. Add in the chicken and cook until it is no longer pink; reserve.
2. Then, sauté the leek until tender and fragrant. Stir in the ginger-garlic paste, poultry seasoning mix, salt, bay leaf, thyme, and rosemary.
3. Pour in the chicken broth and reduce the heat to medium; let it cook for 15 minutes, stirring periodically.
4. Add in the cauliflower and tomatoes along with the reserved bacon and chicken.
5. Decrease the temperature to simmer and let it cook for a further 15 minutes or until warmed through. Bon appétit!

Classic Chicken Parmigiana:

Serves: 2
Preparation Time: 50 minutes
<u>Nutritional information per serving:</u>
Calories: 826
Fat: 50.3 g
Net Carbs: 6.2 g
Protein: 83.2 g
<u>Ingredients:</u>
- 2 pcs boneless chicken thighs
- 8 strips of bacon, chopped
- ½ cup parmesan cheese, grated
- ½ cup mozzarella cheese, shredded
- 1 organic egg
- 1 canned diced tomato

<u>Instructions for Cooking:</u>
1. Set the oven at 450∘ F.
2. Tenderize the chicken and set aside.
3. Place the parmesan cheese on a plate.
4. Crack the egg into a bowl and whisk. And dip the chicken in it.
5. Transfer to the plate with cheese and coat the chicken with the parmesan.
6. Grease the baking sheet with butter, place the chicken thighs and bake in the oven for 30 minutes.
7. While waiting for the chicken to bake, cook the bacon.
8. Pour the tomatoes with the bacon and stir. Reduce the heat to low and allow simmering and reducing.
9. Remove the chicken from the oven when done and ladle over the tomato sauce.
10. Sprinkle with the mozzarella on top and place back in the oven to melt the cheese.
11. Serve hot.

Nutritious Chicken Stir-Fry with Cabbage:

Serves: 2

Preparation Time: 25 minutes

Nutritional information per serving:

Calories: 319

Fat: 18.1 g

Net Carbs: 7 g

Protein: 28.9 g

Ingredients:

- 1/2 lb. chicken breasts, boneless and cut into small pieces
- 2 tablespoons vegetable oil
- 1 yellow onion, chopped
- 2 cloves garlic, sliced
- 3 cups cabbage, shredded
- Salt and pepper, to taste
- 1 teaspoon paprika
- 1 teaspoon lemon juice
- 1 teaspoon basil
- 1 cup vegetable broth
- 1 tablespoon fresh parsley, chopped

Instructions for Cooking:

1. In a large saucepan, heat the vegetable oil over medium heat, then sauté the garlic and onion for 1-2 minutes.
2. Then add the carrot and sliced chicken breasts to the pan and cook for 2-3 minutes.
3. Stir in the shredded cabbage and vegetable broth and mix well.
4. Season with salt, pepper, paprika and basil.
5. Cook for 11-12 minutes or until the cabbage is tender.
6. Drizzle with the lemon juice and stir.
7. Sprinkle with fresh parsley and serve hot.

Sunday Chicken Bake:

Serves: 2

Preparation Time: 30 minutes

<u>Nutritional information per serving:</u>

Calories: 410

Fat: 20.7 g

Net Carbs: 6.2 g

Protein: 50 g

<u>Ingredients:</u>

- 1 tablespoon olive oil
- 3/4 pound chicken breast fillets, chopped into bite-sized chunks
- 2 garlic cloves, sliced
- 1/4 teaspoon Korean chili pepper flakes
- 1/4 teaspoon Himalayan salt
- 1/2 teaspoon poultry seasoning mix
- 1 bell pepper, deveined and chopped
- 2 ripe tomatoes, chopped
- 1/4 cup heavy whipping cream
- 1/4 cup sour cream

<u>Instructions for Cooking:</u>

1. Brush a casserole dish with olive oil. Add the chicken, garlic, Korean chili pepper flakes, salt, and poultry seasoning mix to the casserole dish.
2. Next, layer the pepper and tomatoes. Whisk the heavy whipping cream and sour cream in a mixing bowl.
3. Top everything with the cream mixture.
4. Bake in the preheated oven at 390₀ F for about 25 minutes or until thoroughly heated. Bon appétit!

KETO DIET MEAT RECIPES FOR TWO

Meatballs with Roasted Peppers and Manchego:

Serves: 2

Preparation Time: 1 hour

Nutritional information per serving:

Calories: 348

Fat: 13.7 g

Net Carbs: 5.9 g

Protein: 42.8 g

Ingredients:

- 2 leeks, chopped
- 2 ripe tomatoes, crushed
- 1 pound ground beef
- 1 teaspoon lemon thyme
- 3 garlic cloves
- 1 egg
- 3 tablespoons parmesan cheese, grated
- 1 ½ cups chicken broth
- 1/2 teaspoon fresh ginger, ground
- 4 bell peppers, deveined and chopped
- 2 chipotle peppers, deveined and minced
- 1/2 cup Manchego cheese, crumbled
- Salt and freshly ground black pepper

Instructions for Cooking:

1. Heat -Broil the peppers for about 20 minutes while turning once or twice.
2. Permit them to stand for about a minimum of 30 minutes to loosen the skin.
3. Skin the peppers; get rid of stems and seeds; slice chipotle peppers into equal parts and reserve.
4. In a mixing dish, merge the parmesan, leeks, egg, garlic, salt, pepper, and ground beef. Cook a heavy-bottomed skillet over moderately high heat.
5. Brown meatballs on all sides for about 10 minutes.
6. After the above step, make the tomato sauce. Cook the tomatoes, ginger, chicken broth, and lemon thyme in a pan that is forehead over medium-high heat; spice with salt and pepper to taste.
7. Enable it to boil, reduce the heat to medium. Add meatballs and let them simmer until they are completely cooked, careful stirring.
8. Serve meatballs with the tomato sauce and roasted peppers. Garnish with crumbled Manchego and serve!

Cheddar Zucchini & Beef Mugs:

Serves: 2
Preparation Time: 10 minutes
<u>Nutritional information per serving:</u>
Calories: 188
Fat: 9 g
Net Carbs: 3.7 g
Protein: 18 g
<u>Ingredients:</u>
- 4 oz. roast beef deli slices, torn apart
- 3 tablespoons sour cream
- 1 small zucchini, chopped
- 2 tablespoons chopped green chilies
- 3 oz. shredded cheddar cheese

<u>Instructions for Cooking:</u>
1. Divide the beef slices at the bottom of 2 wide mugs and spread 1 tablespoon of sour cream.
2. Top with 2 zucchini slices, season with salt and pepper, add green chilies, top with the remaining sour cream and then cheddar cheese.
3. Place the mugs in the microwave for 1-2 minutes until the cheese melts.
4. Remove the mugs, let cool for 1 minute, and serve.

Phenomenal Beef Steaks with Fried Onion:

Serves: 2
Preparation Time: 20 minutes
Nutritional information per serving:
Calories: 530
Fat: 35 g
Net Carbs: 3.1 g
Protein: 49.9 g
Ingredients:
- 2 beef sirloin steaks
- 1 teaspoon onion powder
- 1 teaspoon dried oregano
- 1/2 teaspoon salt
- 1 teaspoon dried parsley
- 2 yellow onions, sliced into circles
- 1/3 teaspoon pepper
- 1 teaspoon garlic powder
- 2 tablespoons olive oil
- 1 ½ tablespoons butter

Instructions for Cooking:
1. Preheat the olive oil in a medium skillet over medium heat.
2. Add the onions and cook for 7-8 minutes or until the onions are soft. Stir constantly.
3. Season with salt and pepper. Remove to a large dish and tent with foil.
4. Season the beef steaks with salt, pepper, onion powder, dried oregano, dried parsley, and garlic powder.
5. In a medium pan, preheat the butter. Then add the beef steaks to the pan and fry for 2-3 minutes per side or to the desired doneness.
6. Serve the sirloin steaks and top with the fried onion.

Spicy Habanero and Ground Beef Dinner:

Serves: 2

Preparation Time: 40 minutes

<u>Nutritional information per serving:</u>

Calories: 361

Fat: 21.9 g

Net Carbs: 6.4 g

Protein: 29 g

<u>Ingredients:</u>

- 1/2 teaspoon ground black pepper
- 1/2 teaspoon dried thyme
- 1/2 teaspoon dried basil
- 1 ½ pound ground chuck
- 1 teaspoon habanero pepper, minced
- 1/2 teaspoon ground bay leaf
- 2 tablespoons tallow, at room temperature
- 2 ripe Roma tomatoes, crushed
- 2 shallots, chopped
- 1 teaspoon fennel seeds
- 2 garlic cloves, minced
- 1/4 teaspoon caraway seeds, ground
- 1/2 cup dry sherry wine
- 1/2 teaspoon paprika
- 1/2 teaspoon salt

<u>For Ketogenic Tortillas:</u>

1. A pinch of table salt
2. 4 egg whites
3. A pinch of Swerve
4. 1/3 teaspoon baking powder
5. 1/4 cup coconut flour
6. 6 tablespoons water

<u>Instructions for Cooking:</u>

1. Dissolve the tallow in a wok that is forehead over a normal high heat.
2. Following the above step, brown the ground chuck for a duration of 4 minutes breaking it with a fork.
3. Include all seasonings along with garlic, shallots, and habanero pepper.
4. After that, keep on cooking for an additional 9 minutes.

5. Succeeding the above step, stir in the tomatoes and sherry.
6. Then adjust the heat to medium-low, shut the lid, and let it simmer for a longer period of 20 minutes.
7. In the meantime, prepare the tortillas by mixing the coconut flour, eggs, and baking powder in a container.
8. Add together the salt, water, and Swerve, then mix until everything is well included.
9. Foreheat a nonstick skillet with a moderate flame. Bake tortillas for a notable period of time on each side. Again, repeat until there is no more batter.
10. Enjoy ground beef mixture with warm tortillas.

Bacon Layered Lasagna:

Serves: 2
Preparation Time: 25 minutes
<u>Nutritional information per serving:</u>
Calories: 702
Fat: 41 g
Net Carbs: 10 g
Protein: 75 g
<u>Ingredients:</u>
- 8 bacon strips
- ¼ cup all-natural pizza sauce
- ¼ lb. ground beef
- 1 cup mozzarella cheese, shredded
- 3 tablespoons parmesan cheese, grated
- 1 teaspoon Italian seasoning

<u>Instructions for Cooking:</u>
1. Set oven to 350° F.
2. In a pan, brown the beef over medium heat.
3. Drain the fat from the beef when cooked and then sprinkle with the Italian seasoning.
4. Layer 4 strips of bacon on a 9-inch baking dish and then spread half of the pizza sauce on top.
5. Add half of the ground beef and half of the mozzarella and parmesan and then cover with the remaining pcs. Of bacon and repeat the process.
6. Place in the oven to bake for 12 minutes or until the cheese has melted.

Saucy Pork Cutlets:

Serves: 2
Preparation Time: 25 minutes
Nutritional information per serving:
Calories: 369
Fat: 20.6 g
Net Carbs: 1.1 g
Protein: 40.1 g
Ingredients:
- 1 tablespoon lard, softened at room temperature
- 2 pork cutlets, 2-inch-thick
- 1/3 cup dry red wine
- 2 garlic cloves, sliced
- 1/2 teaspoon whole black peppercorns
- 4 tablespoons flaky salt
- 1 teaspoon juniper berries
- 1/2 teaspoon cayenne pepper

Instructions for Cooking:
1. Melt the lard in a nonstick skillet over a moderate flame.
2. Now, brown the pork cutlets for about 8 minutes, turning them over to ensure even cooking; reserve.
3. Add a splash of wine to deglaze the pan And Stir in the remaining ingredients and continue to cook until fragrant or for a minute or so.
4. Return the pork cutlets to the skillet, continue to cook until the sauce has thickened and everything is heated through about 10 minutes.
5. Serve warm. Bon appétit!

Creamy Pork Loin:

Serves: 2
Preparation Time: 35 minutes
<u>Nutritional information per serving:</u>
Calories: 647
Fat: 39.4 g
Net Carbs: 2.8 g
Protein: 65.4 g
<u>Ingredients:</u>
<u>For Pork Loin:</u>
- 1 teaspoon dried thyme
- 1 teaspoon paprika
- Salt and ground black pepper, as required
- 4 -4-ounces pork loins

<u>For Sauce:</u>
- ½ cup homemade chicken broth
- ¼ cup heavy cream
- 1 teaspoon organic apple cider vinegar
- 1 tablespoon fresh lemon juice
- 1 tablespoon mustard
- 2 tablespoons fresh parsley, chopped

<u>Instructions for Cooking:</u>
1. In a small bowl, mix well thyme, paprika, salt, and black pepper.
2. Coat each pork loin evenly with the thyme mixture.
3. Heat a lightly greased large pan over high heat and sear the pork loins for about 2-3 minutes per side.
4. With a slotted spoon, transfer the pork loins onto a plate.
5. In the same pan, add the broth, heavy cream, and vinegar over medium heat and bring to a gentle simmer.
6. Add the lemon juice and mustard and stir to combine.
7. Stir in the cooked pork loins and simmer, covered partially for about 10 minutes.
8. Garnish with parsley and serve hot.

Pork Sausage Omelet with Mushrooms:

Serves: 2
Preparation Time: 30 minutes
Nutritional information per serving:
Calories: 534
Fat: 43 g
Net Carbs: 2.7 g
Protein: 29 g
Ingredients:

- ¼ cup sliced cremini mushrooms
- 2 tablespoons olive oil
- 2 oz. pork sausage, crumbled
- 1 small white onion, chopped
- 2 tablespoons butter
- 6 eggs
- 2 oz. shredded cheddar cheese

Instructions for Cooking:

1. Heat olive oil in a pan, add in pork sausage, and fry for 10 minutes; set aside.
2. In the same pan sauté the onion and mushrooms, 8 minutes; set aside.
3. Melt the butter over low heat.
4. Meanwhile, crack the eggs into a bowl and beat with some salt and black pepper until smooth and frothy.
5. Pour the eggs into the pan, swirl to spread around and omelet begins to firm, top with pork, mushroom-onion mixture, and cheese.
6. Using a spatula, carefully remove the egg around the edges of the pan and flip over the stuffing, for 2 minutes.
7. Serve warm for breakfast or brunch.

Juicy Pork Chops with Mushrooms:

Serves: 2
Preparation Time: 25 minutes
Nutritional information per serving:
Calories: 512
Fat: 35 g
Net Carbs: 4 g
Protein: 42.1 g
Ingredients:
- 2 pork chops, boneless
- 2 tablespoons vegetable oil
- 2 tablespoons butter
- 1 yellow onion, sliced
- 2 cloves garlic, minced
- 1 cup vegetable broth
- Salt and pepper, to taste
- ½ teaspoon paprika
- 1 cup mushrooms, cut into ½ inch pieces
- 1 tablespoon fresh parsley, chopped

Instructions for Cooking:
1. Heat the oil during a large pan over high heat. Season the pork chops with paprika, salt
2. And pepper.
3. Place the pork chops in the pan and fry for 3-4 minutes per side or until golden brown. Remove from the pan and set aside.
4. In a large skillet add the butter, minced garlic, mushrooms and diced onion. Sauté for 3-4 minutes. Season with salt and pepper. Cook until golden brown.
5. Pour in the vegetable broth and simmer for 5-6 minutes or until the sauce gets thick.
6. Place the pork chops to the skillet and cook for 1 minute more. Sprinkle with fresh parsley and serve immediately.

Creamy Pork Loin Steaks with Spinach Sauce:

Serves: 2
Preparation Time: 20 minutes
<u>Nutritional information per serving:</u>
Calories: 332
Fat: 15.3 g
Net Carbs: 3.2 g
Protein: 43.2 g
<u>Ingredients:</u>

- 2 pork loin steaks
- 2 tablespoons vegetable oil
- 1 teaspoon pepper
- 1/2 cup cream cheese
- 3 tablespoons vegetable broth
- 2 garlic cloves, minced
- 2 cups fresh spinach, washed and chopped
- 1 teaspoon Kosher salt
- 1 teaspoon dried rosemary

<u>Instructions for Cooking:</u>

1. Heat 1 tablespoon of the vegetable oil in a preheated on medium heat pan.
2. Season the pork loin with salt and pepper. Add the pork loin to the pan and cook for 4-5 minutes per side or until browned. Set aside.
3. In a medium saucepan add the remaining vegetable oil and garlic. Fry the garlic for 1 minute and add the spinach.
4. Cook the spinach until it gets wilted and stir in the cream cheese and vegetable broth. Season with Kosher salt, pepper, and dried rosemary.
5. Simmer for 5-6 minutes or until the sauce gets thick. Serve the pork loin topped with the spinach sauce.

Macadamia Crusted Lamb Chops:

Serves: 2

Preparation Time: 30 minutes

<u>Nutritional information per serving:</u>

Calories: 856

Fat: 66 g

Net Carbs: 9.1 g

Protein: 60.3 g

<u>Ingredients:</u>

- 6 pcs lamb chops
- ¾ cup macadamia nuts, ground
- 2 tablespoons fresh rosemary
- Salt and pepper to taste
- 2 tablespoons ghee

<u>Instructions for Cooking:</u>

1. Set oven to 350° F.
2. Season the lamb chops with salt and pepper. Drizzle with ghee on top.
3. Combine the macadamia nuts and rosemary and roll the lamb chops in the mixture.
4. Place the lamb chops on a baking sheet lined with oil and place in the oven to cook for 25 minutes.
5. Serve warm.

KETO DIET SEAFOOD RECIPES FOR TWO

Octopus Salad:

Serves: 2
Preparation Time: 50 minutes
Nutritional information per serving:
Calories: 140
Fat: 10 g
Net Carbs: 6 g
Protein: 23 g
Ingredients:

- 21 ounces octopus; rinsed
- Juice of 1 lemon
- 4 celery stalks; chopped.
- 4 tablespoons parsley; chopped.
- 3 ounces olive oil
- Salt and black pepper to the taste.

Instructions for Cooking:

1. Put the octopus in a pot, add water to cover, cover the pot, bring to a boil over medium heat; cook for 40 minutes, drain and leave aside to cool down.
2. Chop octopus and put it in a salad bowl.
3. Add celery stalks, parsley, oil and lemon juice and toss well.
4. Season with salt and pepper, toss again
5. And serve.

Tasty Shrimp in Creamy Butter Sauce:

Serves: 2

Preparation Time: 30 minutes

<u>Nutritional information per serving:</u>

Calories: 560

Fat: 56 g

Net Carbs: 4.3 g

Protein: 18 g

<u>Ingredients:</u>

- ½ oz. grated Parmesan cheese
- 1 egg, beaten in a bowl
- ¼ teaspoon curry powder
- 2 teaspoons almond flour
- 12 shrimp, shelled
- 3 tablespoons coconut oil
- 2 tablespoons curry leaves
- 2 tablespoons butter
- ½ onion, diced
- ½ cup heavy cream
- ½ ounce cheddar cheese
- Salt and black pepper to taste

<u>Instructions for Cooking:</u>

1. Combine Parmesan, curry powder, and almond flour in a bowl.
2. Melt the copra oil during a skillet over medium heat.
3. Dip the shrimp in the egg first, and then coat with the dry mixture.
4. Fry until golden and crispy. In another skillet, melt the butter Add onion and cook for 3 minutes.
5. Add in curry leaves and cook for 30 seconds. Stir in heavy cream and cheddar cheese and cook until thickened.
6. Add the shrimp and coat well. Adjust the seasoning, and serve.

Pan-Fried Monkfish Medallions with Lemon Sauce:

Serves: 2
Preparation Time: 20 minutes
<u>Nutritional information per serving:</u>
Calories: 328
Fat: 17.5 g
Net Carbs: 3.9 g
Protein: 37.3 g
<u>Ingredients:</u>
- 1 ½ lb. monkfish, cut into medallions
- Salt and pepper, to taste
- 2 tablespoons olive oil
- Lemon wedges, for serving

<u>For the lemon sauce:</u>
- 3 tablespoons butter, melted
- ½ lemon, juiced
- Salt and pepper, to taste
- 1 tablespoon Dijon mustard

<u>Instructions for Cooking:</u>
1. Season the monkfish with salt and pepper.
2. Place a frying pan over medium heat and add the olive oil.
3. Add the monkfish medallions to the pan and cook on both sides until golden brown. Set aside.
4. In a small bowl mix the melted butter, lemon juice, Dijon mustard, salt and pepper. Stir well.
5. Serve the monkfish medallions with the lemon wedges and drizzle with the lemon sauce.

Creole Shrimp:

Serves: 2

Preparation Time: 18 minutes

<u>Nutritional information per serving:</u>

Calories: 120

Fat: 3 g

Net Carbs: 2 g

Protein: 6 g

<u>Ingredients:</u>

- ½ lb. large shrimp, peeled and deveined
- 2 teaspoons Worcestershire sauce
- 2 teaspoons olive oil
- Juice of 1 lemon
- Salt and black pepper to taste
- 1 teaspoon Creole seasoning

<u>Instructions for Cooking:</u>

1. Arrange shrimp on a baking dish, sprinkle with salt and pepper, and drizzle with olive oil.
2. Combine Worcestershire sauce, lemon juice and creole seasoning in a bowl, and drizzle over the shrimp.
3. Toss shrimp a bit to coat, and broil in an oven for 8 minutes.
4. Divide between 2 plates and serve.
5. Enjoy!

Sea Bass with Vegetables and Dill Sauce:

Serves: 2

Preparation Time: 25 minutes

<u>Nutritional information per serving:</u>

Calories: 374

Fat: 17 g

Net Carbs: 6.2 g

Protein: 43.2 g

<u>Ingredients:</u>

- 1 tablespoon olive oil
- 1 cup red onions, sliced
- 2 bell peppers, deveined and sliced
- Sea salt and cayenne pepper, to taste
- 1 teaspoon paprika
- 1 pound sea bass fillets

<u>Dill Sauce:</u>

- 1 tablespoon mayonnaise
- 1/4 cup Greek yogurt
- 1 tablespoon fresh dill, chopped
- 1/2 teaspoon garlic powder
- 1/2 fresh lemon, juiced

<u>Instructions for Cooking:</u>

1. Toss the onions, peppers, and sea bass fillets with olive oil, salt, cayenne pepper, and paprika.
2. Line a baking pan with a piece of parchment paper. Preheat your oven to 400₀ F.
3. Arrange your fish and vegetables on the prepared baking pan. Bake for 10 minutes; turn them over and bake for a further 10 to 12 minutes.
4. Meanwhile, make the sauce by mixing all ingredients until well combined.
5. Serve the fish and vegetables with the dill sauce on the side. Bon appétit!

Scallops and Fennel Sauce Recipe:

Serves: 2
Preparation Time: 20 minutes
<u>Nutritional information per serving:</u>
Calories: 400
Fat: 24 g
Net Carbs: 12 g
Protein: 25 g
<u>Ingredients:</u>

- 1 fennel; trimmed, leaves chopped and bulbs cut into wedges
- Juice of 1/2 lime
- 1 lime; cut into wedges
- 6 scallops
- 3 tablespoons ghee; melted and heated up
- 1/2 tablespoons olive oil
- Zest from 1 lime
- 1 egg yolk
- Salt and black pepper to the taste.

<u>Instructions for Cooking:</u>

1. Season scallops with salt and pepper, put in a bowl and mix with half of the lime juice and half of the zest and toss to coat.
2. In a bowl, mix the egg yolk with some salt and pepper, the rest of the lime juice and the rest of the lime zest and whisk well.
3. Add melted ghee and stir very well.
4. Also, add fennel leaves and stir.
5. Brush fennel wedges with oil, place on heated grill over medium-high heat; cook for 2 minutes, flip and cook for 2 minutes more
6. Add scallops on the grill, cook for 2 minutes, flip and cook for 2 minutes more
7. Divide fennel and scallops on plates, drizzle fennel and ghee mix and serve with lime wedges on the side

Grilled Swordfish:

Serves: 2
Preparation Time: 3 hours 20 minutes
<u>Nutritional information per serving:</u>
Calories: 136
Fat: 5 g
Net Carbs: 1 g
Protein: 20 g
<u>Ingredients:</u>

- 4 swordfish steaks
- 3 garlic cloves; minced
- 1 tablespoon parsley; chopped.
- 1/4 cup lemon juice
- 1 lemon; cut into wedges
- 1/3 cup chicken stock
- 1/2 teaspoon marjoram; dried
- 3 tablespoons olive oil
- 1/2 teaspoon rosemary; dried
- 1/2 teaspoon sage; dried
- Salt and black pepper to the taste.

<u>Instructions for Cooking:</u>

1. In a bowl, mix chicken stock with garlic, lemon juice, olive oil, salt, pepper, sage, marjoram and rosemary and whisk well.
2. Add swordfish steaks, toss to coat and keep in the fridge for 3 hours
3. Place marinated fish steaks on preheated grill over medium high heat and cook for 5 minutes on each side
4. Arrange on plates, sprinkle parsley on to and serve with lemon wedges on the side

Nutty Sea Bass:

Serves: 2
Preparation Time: 30 minutes
<u>Nutritional information per serving:</u>
Calories: 467
Fat: 31 g
Net Carbs: 2.8 g
Protein: 40 g
<u>Ingredients:</u>

- 2 sea bass fillets
- 2 tablespoons butter
- ⅓ Cup roasted hazelnuts
- A pinch of cayenne pepper

<u>Instructions for Cooking:</u>

1. Preheat oven to 420∘ F. Line a baking dish with waxed paper.
2. Melt butter and brush it over the fillets.
3. In a food processor, combine the remaining ingredients.
4. Coat the fish with the hazelnut mixture.
5. Bake for 15 minutes.

Spicy Sushi Roll with Cucumber and Tuna:

Serves: 2

Preparation Time: 10 minutes

<u>Nutritional information per serving:</u>

Calories: 242

Fat: 13.9 g

Net Carbs: 7.9 g

Protein: 21.2 g

<u>Ingredients:</u>

- 1 large cucumber
- 1 can tuna, drained
- 1/3 cup cream cheese
- Salt and pepper, to taste
- ½ teaspoon chili powder
- 1 jalapeno, thinly sliced
- 1 ½ teaspoon sesame seeds

<u>Instructions for Cooking:</u>

1. Cut the cucumber into thin slices with a vegetable peeler.
2. In a small bowl mix the tuna, cream cheese and chili powder. Season with salt and pepper. Stir well.
3. Spread a small amount of the tuna mixture onto the cucumber strips.
4. Then place the jalapeno slices at the end of cucumber strips and roll.
5. Sprinkle with sesame seeds and serve. Bon appetite!

Coconut King Prawns:

Serves: 2
Preparation Time: 4 minutes
<u>Nutritional information per serving:</u>
Calories: 567
Fat: 25.2 g
Net Carbs: 9 g
Protein: 71.3 g
<u>Ingredients:</u>
- 1 tablespoon cloves garlic, peeled & grated
- 1 tablespoon coriander
- 1 tablespoon curry paste -red Thai
- 1 teaspoon cumin
- 1/2 kilogram king prawns, shells removed
- 2 limes, rind & juice
- 3 tablespoons coconut oil
- Salt & pepper

<u>Instructions for Cooking:</u>
1. Put the IP steamer basket in the inner pot and pour 1 cup water.
2. In a mixing bowl, mix the curry paste, coconut oil, garlic, and lime till well mixed.
3. Add the rest of the ingredients to the bowl; toss well to coat the prawns. Put the prawns in the basket.
4. Lock the lid and close the pressure valve. Set to STEAM for 1 minute.
5. QPR when the timer beeps; unlock the lid and open. Shake the prawns.
6. Put in a serving dish. Sprinkle with cumin.
7. Save the cooking water as stock for other dishes.

Hungarian Fish Paprikash (Halászlé):

Serves: 2

Preparation Time: 20 minutes

<u>Nutritional information per serving:</u>

Calories: 252

Fat: 12.6 g

Net Carbs: 5 g

Protein: 1.9 g

<u>Ingredients:</u>

- 1 tablespoon canola oil
- 2 bell peppers, chopped
- 1 Hungarian wax pepper, chopped
- 1 garlic clove, minced
- 1 red onion, chopped
- 1/2 pound tilapia, cut into bite-sized pieces
- 1 ½ cups fish broth
- 2 vine-ripe tomatoes, pureed
- 1 teaspoon sweet paprika
- 1/2 teaspoon mixed peppercorns, crushed
- 1 bay laurel
- 1/2 teaspoon sumac
- 1/2 teaspoon dried thyme
- 1/4 teaspoon dried rosemary
- Kosher salt, to season
- 1/2 teaspoon garlic, minced
- 2 tablespoons sour cream

<u>Instructions for Cooking:</u>

1. Heat the canola oil in a Dutch oven over medium-high heat.
2. Now, sauté the peppers, garlic, and onion until tender and aromatic.
3. Now, stir in the tilapia, broth, tomatoes, and spices. Reduce the heat to medium-low. Let it simmer, covered, for 9 to 13 minutes.
4. Meanwhile, mix 1/2 teaspoon of minced garlic with the sour cream. Serve with the warm paprikash and enjoy it!

KETO DIET SOUPS RECIPES FOR TWO

Warming Turkey and Leek Soup:

Serves: 2
Preparation Time: 1 hour 15 minutes
Nutritional information per serving:
Calories: 216
Fat: 8.1 g
Net Carbs: 6.8 g
Protein: 25.2 g
Ingredients:

- 3 cups of water
- 1/2 pound turkey thighs
- 1 cup cauliflower, broken into small florets
- 1 large-sized leek, chopped
- 1 small-sized stalk celery, chopped
- 1/2 head garlic, split horizontally
- 1/4 teaspoon turmeric powder
- 1/4 teaspoon Turkish sumac
- 1/4 teaspoon fennel seeds
- 1/2 teaspoon mustard seeds
- 1 bay laurel
- Sea salt and freshly ground black pepper, to season
- 1 teaspoon coconut aminos
- 1 whole egg

Instructions for Cooking:

1. Add the water and turkey thighs to a pot and bring it to a rolling boil.
2. Cook for about 40 minutes; discard the bones and shred the meat using two forks.
3. Stir in the cauliflower, leeks, celery, garlic, and spices. Reduce the heat to simmer and let it cook until everything is heated through about 30 minutes.
4. Afterward, add the coconut aminos and egg; whisk until the egg is well incorporated into the soup.
5. Serve hot and enjoy!

Chinese Tofu Soup:

Serves: 2
Preparation Time: 15 minutes
<u>Nutritional information per serving:</u>
Calories: 163
Fat: 10 g
Net Carbs: 2.4 g
Protein: 14.5 g
<u>Ingredients:</u>

- 2 cups chicken stock
- 1 tablespoon soy sauce, sugar-free
- 2 spring onions, sliced
- 1 teaspoon sesame oil, softened
- 2 eggs, beaten
- 1-inch piece ginger, grated
- Salt and black ground, to taste
- ½ pound extra-firm tofu, cubed
- A handful of fresh cilantro, chopped

<u>Instructions for Cooking:</u>

1. Boil in a pan over medium heat, soy sauce, chicken stock and sesame oil.
2. Place in eggs as you whisk to incorporate completely.
3. Change heat to low and add salt, spring onions, black pepper and ginger; cook for 5 minutes.
4. Place in tofu and simmer for 1 to 2 minutes.
5. Divide into soup bowls and serve sprinkled with fresh cilantro.

Awesome Chicken Enchilada Soup:

Serves: 4
Preparation Time: 30 minutes
<u>Nutritional information per serving:</u>
Calories: 643
Fat: 44.2 g
Net Carbs: 9.7 g
Protein: 45.8 g
<u>Ingredients:</u>

- 2 tablespoons coconut oil
- 1 lb. boneless, skinless chicken thighs
- ¾ cup red enchilada sauce, sugar-free
- ¼ cup of water
- ¼ cup onion, chopped
- 3 oz. canned diced green chilis
- 1 avocado, sliced
- 1 cup cheddar cheese, shredded
- ¼ cup pickled jalapeños, chopped
- ½ cup sour cream
- 1 tomato, diced

<u>Instructions for Cooking:</u>

1. Put a large pan over medium heat. Add coconut oil and warm.
2. Place in the chicken and cook until browned on the outside.
3. Stir in onion, chillis, water, and enchilada sauce, then close with a lid.
4. Allow simmering for 20 minutes until the chicken is cooked through.
5. Spoon the soup on a serving bowl and top with the sauce, cheese, sour cream, tomato, and avocado.

CHICKEN VEGETABLE SOUP:

Serves: 2
Preparation Time: 10 minutes
Nutritional information per serving:
Calories: 120
Fat: 4 g
Net Carbs: 11 g
Protein: 10 g
Ingredients:

- 2 quarts chicken bouillon
- 1 cup sliced carrots
- 1 cup fresh or frozen green peas
- 1 cup chopped celery
- 1 teaspoons salt
- 2 cups diced cooked chicken
- 1 teaspoon dried whole rosemary
- 1 teaspoon dried whole thyme

Instructions for Cooking:

1. Combine the first 5 ingredients in a large Dutch oven; bring to a boil.
2. Stir in remaining ingredients. Reduce heat; cover and simmer 15 minutes or until vegetables are tender.

Chilled Cucumber Soup:

Serves: 2
Preparation Time: 15 minutes
<u>Nutritional information per serving:</u>
Calories: 289
Fat: 28.7 g
Net Carbs: 5.6 g
Protein: 3.4 g
<u>Ingredients:</u>

- 1 cup English cucumber, peeled and chopped
- 1 scallion, chopped
- 2 tablespoons fresh parsley leaves
- 2 tablespoons fresh basil leaves
- ¼ teaspoon fresh lime zest, grated freshly
- 1 cup unsweetened coconut milk
- ¼ cup of water
- ½ tablespoon fresh lime juice
- Salt and ground black pepper, as required

<u>Instructions for Cooking:</u>

1. Add all the ingredients in a high-speed blender and pulse on high speed until smooth.
2. Transfer the soup into a large serving bowl.
3. Cover the bowl and refrigerate to chill for about 6 hours.
4. Serve chilled.

Curried Shrimp & Green Bean Soup:

Serves: 4
Preparation Time: 20 minutes
<u>Nutritional information per serving:</u>
Calories: 351
Fat: 32.4 g
Net Carbs: 3.2 g
Protein: 7.7 g
<u>Ingredients:</u>

- 1 onion, chopped
- 2 tablespoons red curry paste
- 2 tablespoons butter
- 1 pound jumbo shrimp, peeled and deveined
- 2 teaspoons ginger-garlic puree
- 1 cup of coconut milk
- Salt and chili pepper to taste
- 1 bunch green beans, halved
- 1 tablespoon cilantro, chopped

<u>Instructions for Cooking:</u>

1. Add the shrimp to melted butter in a saucepan over medium heat, season with salt and pepper, and cook until they are opaque, 2 to 3 minutes.
2. Remove to a plate. Add in the ginger-garlic puree, onion, and red curry paste and sauté for 2 minutes until fragrant.
3. Stir in the coconut milk; add the shrimp, salt, chili pepper, and green beans.
4. Cook for 4 minutes. Reduce the heat to a simmer and cook an additional 3 minutes, occasionally stirring.
5. Adjust taste with salt, fetch soup into serving bowls, and serve sprinkled with cilantro.

Mushroom Cream Soup with Herbs:

Serves: 4
Preparation Time: 25 minutes
Nutritional information per serving:
Calories: 213
Fat: 18 g
Net Carbs: 4.1 g
Protein: 3.1 g
Ingredients:

- 1 onion, chopped
- ½ cup crème Fraiche
- ¼ cup butter
- 12 oz. white mushrooms, chopped
- 1 teaspoon thyme leaves, chopped
- 1 teaspoon parsley leaves, chopped
- 1 teaspoon cilantro leaves, chopped
- 2 garlic cloves, minced
- 4 cups vegetable broth
- Salt and black pepper, to taste

Instructions for Cooking:

1. Add butter, onion and garlic to a large pot over high heat and cook for 3 minutes until tender.
2. Add mushrooms, salt and pepper, and cook for 10 minutes.
3. Pour in the broth and bring to a boil And Reduce the heat and simmer for 10 minutes And Puree the soup with a hand blender until smooth.
4. Stir in crème Fraiche. Garnish with herbs before serving.

Vegan Approved Spinach and Lentil Soup:

Serves: 4

Preparation Time: 30minutes

<u>Nutritional information per serving:</u>

Calories: 270.9

Fat: 1 g

Net Carbs: 42.8 g

Protein: 13 g

<u>Ingredients:</u>

- 8 oz. baby spinach
- 4 cups low-sodium vegetable broth
- 1 cup dry brown lentils, rinsed
- ¼ teaspoon ground pepper
- 1 teaspoon dried thyme
- 1 teaspoon ground turmeric
- 2 teaspoons ground cumin
- 4 medium garlic cloves, minced
- 1 medium stalk celery, diced
- 2 medium carrots, peeled and diced
- ½ medium yellow onion, diced
- 1 teaspoon olive oil

<u>Instructions for Cooking:</u>

1. Place a heavy-bottomed pot on medium-high fire and heat pot for 3 minutes.
2. Once hot, add oil and stir around to coat pot with oil.
3. Stir in celery, carrots, onions, and garlic. Sauté for 5 minutes.
4. Stir in pepper, thyme, and cumin. Sauté for a minute.
5. Add broth and lentils. Mix well.
6. Cover, bring to a boil, lower fire to a simmer and simmer for 15 minutes.
7. Stir in spinach, turn off fie, and let it sit for 3 minutes or until spinach is wilted.
8. Serve and enjoy.

Broccoli & Spinach Soup:

Serves: 2
Preparation Time: 25 minutes
<u>Nutritional information per serving:</u>
Calories: 123
Fat: 11 g
Net Carbs: 3.2 g
Protein: 1.8 g
<u>Ingredients:</u>

- 2 tablespoons butter
- 1 onion, chopped
- 1 garlic clove, minced
- 2 heads broccoli, cut in florets
- 2 stalks celery, chopped
- 4 cups vegetable broth
- 1 cup baby spinach
- Salt and black pepper to taste
- 1 tablespoon basil, chopped
- Parmesan cheese shaved to serve

<u>Instructions for Cooking:</u>

1. Melt the butter in a saucepan over medium heat And Sauté the garlic and onion for 3 minutes until softened.
2. Mix in the broccoli and celery, and cook for 4 minutes until slightly tender.
3. Pour in the broth, bring to a boil, then reduce the heat to medium-low and simmer covered for about 5 minutes.
4. Drop in the spinach to wilt, adjust the seasonings, and cook for 4 minutes.
5. Ladle soup into serving bowls.
6. Serve with a sprinkle of grated Parmesan cheese and chopped basil.

Tomato Cream Soup with Basil:

Serves: 4

Preparation Time: 20 minutes

<u>Nutritional information per serving:</u>

Calories: 253

Fat: 23.5 g

Net Carbs: 6.2 g

Protein: 4.1 g

<u>Ingredients:</u>

- 1 carrot, chopped
- 2 tablespoons olive oil
- 1 onion, diced
- 1 garlic clove, minced
- ¼ cup raw cashew nuts, diced
- 14 ounces canned tomatoes
- 1 teaspoon fresh basil leaves + extra to garnish
- 1 cup of water
- Salt and black pepper to taste
- 1 cup crème fraîche

<u>Instructions for Cooking:</u>

1. Warm olive oil in a pot over medium heat and sauté the onion, carrot, and garlic for 4 minutes until softened.
2. Stir in the tomatoes, basil, water, cashew nuts, and season with salt and black pepper.
3. Cover and bring to simmer for 10 minutes until thoroughly cooked.
4. Puree the ingredients with an immersion blender. Adjust to taste and stir in the crème fraîche.
5. Serve sprinkled with basil.

Awesome Chicken Enchilada Soup:

Serves: 4
Preparation Time: 30 minutes
<u>Nutritional information per serving:</u>
Calories: 643
Fat: 44.2 g
Net Carbs: 9.7 g
Protein: 45.8 g
<u>Ingredients:</u>

- 2 tablespoons coconut oil
- 1 lb. boneless, skinless chicken thighs
- ¾ cup red enchilada sauce, sugar-free
- ¼ cup of water
- ¼ cup onion, chopped
- 3 oz. canned diced green chilis
- 1 avocado, sliced
- 1 cup cheddar cheese, shredded
- ¼ cup pickled jalapeños, chopped
- ½ cup sour cream
- 1 tomato, diced

<u>Instructions for Cooking:</u>

1. Put a large pan over medium heat.
2. Add coconut oil and warm. Place in the chicken and cook until browned on the outside.
3. Stir in onion, chillis, water, and enchilada sauce, then close with a lid.
4. Allow simmering for 20 minutes until the chicken is cooked through.
5. Spoon the soup on a serving bowl and top with the sauce, cheese, sour cream, tomato, and avocado.

KETO DIET SIDES DISHES RECIPES FOR TWO

Fried Swiss Chard:

Serves: 2
Preparation Time: 20 minutes
Nutritional information per serving:
Calories: 300
Fat: 32 g
Net Carbs: 6 g
Protein: 8 g
Ingredients:
- 4 bacon slices, chopped.
- 2 tablespoons ghee
- 1/2 teaspoon garlic paste
- 1 bunch Swiss chard, roughly chopped.
- 3 tablespoons lemon juice
- Salt and black pepper to the taste.

Instructions for Cooking:
1. Heat up a pan over medium heat; add bacon pieces and cook until it's crispy.
2. Add ghee and stir until it melts
3. Add garlic paste and lemon juice; stir and cook for 1 minute
4. Add Swiss chard; stir and cook for 4 minutes
5. Add salt and black pepper to the taste; stir, divide between plates and serve as a keto side dish.

Stuffed Portobello Mushrooms:

Serves: 2
Preparation Time: 30 minutes
Nutritional information per serving:
Calories: 334
Fat: 5.5 g
Net Carbs: 29 g
Protein: 14 g
Ingredients:

- 4 Portobello mushrooms
- 2 tablespoons olive oil
- 2 cups lettuce
- 1 cup crumbled blue cheese

Instructions for Cooking:

1. Preheat oven to 350° F.
2. Remove the stems from the mushrooms.
3. Fill the mushrooms with blue cheese and place them on a lined baking sheet.
4. Bake for about 20 minutes.
5. Serve with lettuce drizzled with olive oil.

Ordinary Brussel Sprouts with Cheddar:

Serves: 2

Preparation Time: 15 minutes

<u>Nutritional information per serving:</u>

Calories: 288

Fat: 23.4 g

Net Carbs: 7 g

Protein: 10.8 g

<u>Ingredients:</u>

- 2 tablespoons olive oil
- 12 Brussel sprouts halved
- 3 tablespoons cheddar cheese, grated
- ½ teaspoon paprika
- 1/3 teaspoon salt
- 1/3 teaspoon pepper

<u>Instructions for Cooking:</u>

1. Preheat the oven to 350◦ F and line a large baking dish lined with parchment paper.
2. Place the Brussel sprouts on the parchment paper. Drizzle with the olive oil and season with salt, pepper, and paprika.
3. Bake the Brussel sprouts for 15 minutes or until crispy. Sprinkle with the shredded cheddar cheese and serve hot.

Winter Keto Oatmeal:

Serves: 2
Preparation Time: 10 minutes
<u>Nutritional information per serving:</u>
Calories: 352
Fat: 34.8 g
Net Carbs: 6.3 g
Protein: 5.5 g
<u>Ingredients:</u>

- 3 tablespoons pumpkin seeds
- 1 tablespoon chia seeds
- 1 tablespoon sunflower seeds
- Himalayan salt, to taste
- 2 tablespoons coconut oil
- 1/2 cup coconut milk
- 1/2 cup water
- 1 teaspoon ground cinnamon
- 1 teaspoon vanilla paste
- 1/2 teaspoons granulated stevia

<u>Instructions for Cooking:</u>

1. Place all ingredients in your Instant Pot.
2. Secure the lid. Choose "Manual" mode and High pressure; cook for 5 minutes.
3. Once cooking is complete, use a quick pressure release; carefully remove the lid.
4. Divide between two bowls and serve hot. Enjoy!!

Italian-Style Asparagus with Cheese:

Serves: 2

Preparation Time: 10 minutes

Nutritional information per serving:

Calories: 193

Fat: 14.1 g

Net Carbs: 5.6 g

Protein: 11.5 g

Ingredients:

- 1/2 pound asparagus spears, trimmed, cut into bite-sized pieces
- 1 teaspoon Italian spice blend
- 1/2 tablespoon lemon juice
- 1 tablespoon extra-virgin olive oil
- 4 tablespoons Romano cheese, freshly grated

Instructions for Cooking:

1. Bring a saucepan of lightly salted water to a boil.
2. Turn the heat to medium-low. Add the asparagus spears and cook approximately 3 minutes.
3. Drain and transfer to a serving bowl.
4. Add the Italian spice blend, lemon juice, and extra-virgin olive oil; toss until well coated.
5. Top with Romano cheese and serve immediately. Bon appétit!

Spinach Side Dish:

Serves: 2
Preparation Time: 25 minutes
<u>Nutritional information per serving:</u>
Calories: 133
Fat: 10 g
Net Carbs: 4 g
Protein: 2 g
<u>Ingredients:</u>

- 2 garlic cloves, minced
- 8 ounces of spinach leaves
- 4 tablespoons sour cream
- 1 tablespoon ghee
- 2 tablespoons parmesan cheese, grated
- A drizzle of olive oil
- Salt and black pepper to the taste.

<u>Instructions for Cooking:</u>

1. Heat up a pan with the oil over medium heat; add spinach; stir and cook until it softens.
2. Add salt, pepper, ghee, parmesan and ghee; stir and cook for 4 minutes.
3. Add sour cream; stir and cook for 5 minutes more.
4. Divide between plates and serve as a side dish.

Vegetarian Ketogenic Burgers:

Serves: 2
Preparation Time: 20 minutes
<u>Nutritional information per serving:</u>
Calories: 637
Fat: 53 g
Net Carbs: 8.5 g
Protein: 23 g
<u>Ingredients:</u>

- 1 garlic cloves, minced
- 2 Portobello mushrooms
- 1 tablespoon coconut oil, melted
- 1 tablespoon chopped basil
- 1 tablespoon oregano
- 2 eggs, fried
- 2 zero carb buns
- 2 tablespoons mayonnaise
- 2 lettuce leaves
- Salt to taste

<u>Instructions for Cooking:</u>

1. Combine the melted coconut oil, garlic, herbs, and salt in a bowl.
2. Place the mushrooms in the bowl and coat well.
3. Preheat the grill to medium. Grill the mushrooms about 2 minutes per side.
4. Slice them and grill for 2 minutes per side. Cut the buns in half.
5. Add the lettuce leaves, mushrooms, eggs, and mayo.
6. Top with the other bun.

Tuna Salad with Lettuce & Olives:

Serves: 2

Preparation Time: 5 minutes

Nutritional information per serving:

Calories: 248

Fat: 20 g

Net Carbs: 2 g

Protein: 18.5 g

Ingredients:

- 1 cup of canned tuna, drained
- 1 teaspoon onion flakes
- 3 tablespoons mayonnaise
- 1 cup shredded romaine lettuce
- 1 tablespoon lime juice
- Sea salt, to taste
- 6 black olives, pitted and sliced

Instructions for Cooking:

1. Combine the tuna, mayonnaise, lime juice, and salt in a small bowl; mix to combine well.
2. In a salad platter, arrange the shredded lettuce and onion flakes.
3. Spread the tuna mixture over; top with black olives to serve.

Roasted Portobellos with Edam and Herbs:

Serves: 2

Preparation Time: 45 minutes

Nutritional information per serving:

Calories: 308

Fat: 24.1 g

Net Carbs: 6.1 g

Protein: 17.9 g

Ingredients:

- 2 tablespoons ghee, melted
- 1 pound white portobello mushrooms, cleaned and sliced
- 1/4 teaspoon smoked paprika
- 1/2 teaspoon cayenne pepper
- 1/4 teaspoon black pepper, cracked
- 1/2 teaspoon dried oregano
- 1/2 teaspoon dried basil
- Sea salt, to taste
- 3 ounces Edam cheese, shredded
- 1 tablespoon fresh cilantro, chopped
- 1/2 tablespoon fresh tarragon, chopped

Instructions for Cooking:

1. Drizzle the melted ghee over your portobellos.
2. Sprinkle the smoked paprika, cayenne pepper, black pepper, oregano, basil, and salt over your mushrooms.
3. Roast in the preheated oven at 370₀ F for about 35 minutes or until they have softened; at the halfway point, turn them over to ensure even cooking.
4. Scatter the Edam cheese over your mushrooms and roast an additional 4 to 5 minutes or until it is bubbling.
5. Serve warm, garnished with fresh cilantro and tarragon. Bon appétit!

Strawberry Faux Oats:

Serves: 2
Preparation Time: 20 minutes
<u>Nutritional information per serving:</u>
Calories: 289
Fat: 18 g
Net Carbs: 6 g
Protein: 5 g
<u>Ingredients:</u>

- 2 tablespoons coconut flour
- 2 tablespoons golden flaxseed meal
- 2 tablespoons chia seeds
- 2 tablespoons heavy cream
- ½ cup almond milk
- 3 tablespoons sugar-free maple syrup
- 1 teaspoon vanilla extract
- 1 cup strawberries, halved
- ¼ cup desiccated coconut

<u>Instructions for Cooking:</u>

1. Combine coconut flour, flaxseed meal, and chia seeds in a saucepan.
2. Stir in heavy cream, almond milk, maple syrup, and vanilla extract.
3. Place the pan over medium heat, whisk the ingredients for 10 minutes.
4. Pour the mixture into 2 serving bowls and top with strawberries and desiccated coconut.
5. Drizzle with some more maple syrup and serve.

Caprese Asparagus Salad:

Serves: 2
Preparation Time: 20 minutes
<u>Nutritional information per serving:</u>
Calories: 187
Fat: 13.3 g
Net Carbs: 7.4 g
Protein: 9.5 g
<u>Ingredients:</u>

- 1 teaspoon fresh lime juice
- 1 tablespoon hot Hungarian paprika infused oil
- 1/2 teaspoon kosher salt
- 1/4 teaspoon red pepper flakes
- 1/2 pound asparagus spears, trimmed
- 1 cup grape tomatoes, halved
- 2 tablespoons red wine vinegar
- 1 garlic clove, pressed
- 1-2 drops liquid stevia
- 1 tablespoon fresh basil
- 1 tablespoon fresh chives
- 1/2 cup mozzarella, grated

<u>Instructions for Cooking:</u>

1. Heat your grill to the hottest setting.
2. Toss your asparagus with the lime juice, hot Hungarian paprika infused oil, salt, and red pepper flakes.
3. Place the asparagus spears on the hot grill. Grill until one side chars; then, grill your asparagus on the other side.
4. Cut the asparagus spears into bite-sized pieces and transfer to a salad bowl. Add the grape tomatoes, red wine, garlic, stevia, basil, and chives; toss to combine well.
5. Top with freshly grated mozzarella cheese and serve immediately.

Italian-Style Stuffed Peppers:

Serves: 2
Preparation Time: 30 minutes
<u>Nutritional information per serving:</u>
Calories: 313
Fat: 21.3 g
Net Carbs: 5.7 g
Protein: 20.2 g
<u>Ingredients:</u>

- 1 tablespoon canola oil
- 1 garlic clove, pressed
- 1/2 cup celery, finely chopped
- 1/2 Spanish onion, finely chopped
- 4 ounces pork, ground
- Sea salt, to taste
- 1 teaspoon Italian seasoning mix
- 2 sweet Italian peppers, deveined and halved
- 1 large-sized Roma tomato, pureed
- 1/2 cups cheddar cheese, grated

<u>Instructions for Cooking:</u>

1. Heat the vegetable oil during a sauté pan over medium-high heat.
2. Now, sauté the garlic, celery, and onion until they have softened.
3. Stir in the ground pork and cook for a further 3 minutes or until no longer pink.
4. Sprinkle with salt and Italian seasoning mix. Divide the filling mixture between the pepper halves.
5. Add the pureed tomato to a lightly greased baking dish; place the stuffed peppers in the baking dish.
6. Bake in the preheated oven at 390 degrees F for 20 minutes.
7. Top with the cheddar cheese and bake an additional 4 to 6 minutes or until the cheese is bubbling.
8. Serve warm and enjoy!

KETO DIET SMOOTHIES RECIPES FOR TWO

Fruity Tofu Smoothie:

Serves: 2
Preparation Time: 5 minutes
Nutritional information per serving:
Calories: 175
Fat: 3.7 g
Net Carbs: 33.3 g
Protein: 6 g
Ingredients:

- 1 container silken tofu
- 1 cup packed spinach
- ½ cups frozen pineapple chunks
- 1 medium banana, frozen
- ¼ cups mango chunks, frozen
- 1 cup ice-cold water
- 1 tablespoon chia seeds

Instructions for Cooking:

1. In a powerful blender, add all ingredients and puree until smooth and creamy.
2. Evenly divide into two glasses, serve and enjoy.

Dark Chocolate Smoothie:

Serves: 2
Preparation Time: 10 minutes
<u>Nutritional information per serving:</u>
Calories: 335
Fat: 31.7 g
Net Carbs: 12.7 g
Protein: 7 g
<u>Ingredients:</u>
- 8 pecans
- ¾ cup of coconut milk
- ¼ cup of water
- 1 ½ cups watercress
- 2 teaspoons vegan protein powder
- 1 tablespoon chia seeds
- 1 tablespoon unsweetened cocoa powder
- 4 fresh dates, pitted

<u>Instructions for Cooking:</u>
1. In a blender, add all ingredients and process until creamy and uniform.
2. Place into two glasses and chill to serve.

Power Green Smoothie:

Serves: 2

Preparation Time: 5 minutes

<u>Nutritional information per serving:</u>

Calories: 187

Fat: 12 g

Net Carbs: 7.6 g

Protein: 3.2 g

<u>Ingredients:</u>

- 1 cup collard greens, chopped
- 3 stalks celery, chopped
- 1 ripe avocado, skinned, pitted, sliced
- 1 cup of ice cubes
- 2 cups spinach, chopped
- 1 large cucumber, peeled and chopped
- Chia seeds to garnish

<u>Instructions for Cooking:</u>

1. Add the collard greens, celery, avocado, and ice cubes in a blender, and blend for 50 seconds.
2. Add the spinach and cucumber, and process for another 40 seconds until smooth.
3. Transfer the smoothie into glasses, garnish with chia seeds and serve right away.

KETO STRAWBERRY SMOOTHIE:

Serves: 2
Preparation Time: 5 minutes
Nutritional information per serving:
Calories: 152
Fat: 13 g
Net Carbs: 5 g
Protein: 1 g
Ingredients:
- ¼ cups heavy whipping cream
- ¾ cups unsweetened original almond milk
- 2 teaspoons granulated stevia/erythritol blend (Pyure)
- 4 oz. frozen strawberries
- ½ cup ice
- ½ teaspoon vanilla extract

Instructions for Cooking:
1. Place all ingredients in the blender. Pulse until blended, if necessary, scraping down the sides.
2. Serve in 2 large glasses.

Raspberry Smoothie:

Serves: 2

Preparation Time: 10 minutes

Nutritional information per serving:

Calories: 113

Fat: 9.7 g

Net Carbs: 3 g

Protein: 1.7 g

Ingredients:

- ½ cup fresh raspberries
- ¼ cup heavy whipping cream
- 1 tablespoon cream cheese
- 2 tablespoons Erythritol
- ½ teaspoon organic vanilla extract
- Pinch of salt
- 1¼ cups unsweetened almond milk
- ½ cups of ice cubes

Instructions for Cooking:

1. Place all the ingredients in a high-speed blender and pulse until smooth.
2. Pour the smoothie into serving glasses and serve.

Berry-Banana Yogurt Smoothie:

Serves: 2

Preparation Time: 5 minutes

<u>Nutritional information per serving:</u>

Calories: 183.5

Fat: 2.3 g

Net Carbs: 37 g

Protein: 3.7 g

<u>Ingredients:</u>

- 5-6 ice cubes
- ½ cups blueberries, frozen
- ½ banana, frozen
- 1 container 5.3oz non-fat Greek yogurt
- ¼ cups quick-cooking oats
- 1 cup almond milk
- ¼ cups of chopped Collard Greens, middle stem removed and discarded

<u>Instructions for Cooking:</u>

1. In a microwave-safe cup, microwave on high for 2.5 minutes the 1 cup almond milk and ¼ cups oats.
2. Once oats are cooked, add 2 ice cubes to cool it down quickly and mix.
3. Then pour the rest of the ingredients, along with the slightly cool oat mixture, in a blender and puree until the mixture is smooth and creamy.
4. Serve and enjoy.

Kiwi Coconut Smoothie:

Serves: 2

Preparation Time: 3 minutes

<u>Nutritional information per serving:</u>

Calories: 423

Fat: 35.7 g

Net Carbs: 9.2 g

Protein: 14 g

<u>Ingredients:</u>

- 2 kiwis, pulp scooped
- 1 tablespoon xylitol
- 4 ice cubes
- 2 cups unsweetened coconut milk
- 1 cup of coconut yogurt
- Mint leaves to garnish

<u>Instructions for Cooking:</u>

1. Process the kiwis, xylitol, coconut milk, yogurt, and ice cubes in a blender, until smooth, for about 3 minutes.
2. Transfer to serving glasses, garnish with mint leaves and serve.

Blueberry Smoothie:

Serves: 2
Preparation Time: 10 minutes
<u>Nutritional information per serving:</u>
Calories: 92
Fat: 7.9 g
Net Carbs: 5.1 g
Protein: 1.2 g
<u>Ingredients:</u>

- ½ cups fresh blueberries
- 2 teaspoons MCT oil
- ½ teaspoon organic vanilla extract
- 2-4 drops liquid stevia
- 1¾ cups unsweetened almond milk
- ½ cup of ice cubes

<u>Instructions for Cooking:</u>

1. Add all the ingredients in a high-speed blender and pulse until smooth.
2. Pour the smoothie into serving glasses and serve.

(Tip: For a thicker smoothie, you can add 2-3 tablespoons of yogurt.)

Berry Green and Leafy Smoothie:

Serves: 2
Preparation Time: 5 minutes
Nutritional information per serving:
Calories: 262.5
Fat: 4.9 g
Net Carbs: 49.5 g
Protein: 5.1 g
Ingredients:
- 8 oz. filtered water
- 1 tablespoon ground flax seeds
- 1 cup green leaf lettuce, chopped
- 2 cups chopped dandelion greens
- 8 large strawberries, frozen
- 1 large mango, peeled and pitted
- 1 medium banana, peeled and frozen

Instructions for Cooking:
1. Blend all ingredients during a blender until smooth and creamy.
2. Serve and enjoy.

Vanilla Smoothie:

Serves: 2
Preparation Time: 5 minutes
<u>Nutritional information per serving:</u>
Calories: 369
Fat: 22.7 g
Net Carbs: 6 g
Protein: 34.7 g
<u>Ingredients:</u>
- ½ cups unsweetened vanilla whey protein powder
- 4 tablespoons almond butter
- 2 teaspoons organic vanilla extract
- 6-8 drops liquid stevia
- 2 cups unsweetened almond milk
- ½ cups of ice cubes

<u>Instructions for Cooking:</u>
1. Place all the ingredients in a high-speed blender and pulse until smooth.
2. Pour the smoothie into serving glasses and serve.

(Tip: Be sure to use high quality and unsweetened protein powder.)

Grape-Avocado Smoothie:

Serves: 2

Preparation Time: 5 minutes

Nutritional information per serving:

Calories: 188.8

Fat: 5.2 g

Net Carbs: 20 g

Protein: 15.5 g

Ingredients:

- 1 tablespoon lime juice, fresh
- 2 tablespoons avocado
- 6-oz Greek yogurt, plain
- 15 pcs red or green grapes
- 1 pear, peeled, cored and chopped
- 2 cups packed spinach leaves
- 6 ice cubes

Instructions for Cooking:

1. Blend all ingredients in a blender until smooth
2. And creamy.
3. Serve and enjoy.

KETO DIET DESSERTS RECIPES FOR TWO

Chocolate Mug Cakes:

Serves: 2

Preparation Time: 5 minutes

Nutritional information per serving:

Calories: 92

Fat: 12 g

Net Carbs: 1.8 g

Protein: 8.2 g

Ingredients:

- 2 tablespoons ghee
- 1 ½ tablespoon cocoa powder
- 2-3 tablespoons erythritol
- 1 egg
- 2 tablespoons almond flour
- 1 tablespoon psyllium husk powder
- 2 teaspoons coconut flour
- ½ teaspoon baking powder
- A pinch of salt

Instructions for Cooking:

1. In a bowl, whisk the butter, cocoa powder, and erythritol until a thick mixture forms.
2. Whisk in the egg until smooth and then the almond flour, psyllium husk, coconut flour, baking powder and salt.
3. Pour the mixture into two medium mugs and microwave for 70 to 90 seconds or until set.

Coconut Chia Pudding:

Serves: 2

Preparation Time: 10 minutes

<u>Nutritional information per serving:</u>

Calories: 225

Fat: 20.3 g

Net Carbs: 7.7 g

Protein: 3.8 g

<u>Ingredients:</u>

- 4 tablespoons chia seeds
- 1/2 teaspoon vanilla paste
- 1/4 teaspoon ground cinnamon
- 3/4 cup coconut milk
- 2 tablespoons Swerve
- 2 tablespoons shredded coconut, unsweetened

<u>Instructions for Cooking:</u>

1. Mix all of the ingredients, except for the shredded coconut.
2. Then, place your pudding in a storage container.
3. Cover and let it sit in your refrigerator overnight. Divide the pudding between two serving bowls.
4. Top with the shredded coconut and serve. Devour!

Raspberry Yogurt Parfait:

Serves: 2
Preparation Time: 5 minutes
<u>Nutritional information per serving:</u>
Calories: 183
Fat: 10 g
Net Carbs: 8.9 g
Protein: 7.8 g
<u>Ingredients:</u>

- 1 cup Greek yogurt
- 1 cup fresh raspberries
- ½ lemon, zested
- 3-minute sprigs leave extracted and chopped
- 2 tablespoons chia seeds
- 2 drops liquid stevia

<u>Instructions for Cooking:</u>

1. In a small bowl, whisk the Greek yogurt with stevia.
2. In medium serving glasses, layer half of the Greek yogurt, raspberries, lemon zest, mint, chia seeds, and drizzle with maple syrup.
3. Repeat with another layer. Serve cold.

PEANUT BUTTER CHOCOLATE:

Serves: 2
Preparation Time: 10 minutes
Nutritional information per serving:
Calories: 126.3
Fat: 12.4 g
Net Carbs: 3.3 g
Protein: 3.9 g
Ingredients:

- ½ cups Lily's Dark Chocolate Chips
- 2 tablespoons Lily's sugar-free chocolate chips
- 2 tablespoons peanut butter, creamy of course
- 3 drops of liquid stevia
- 1 pinch of salt

Instructions for Cooking:

1. Heat the dark chocolate chips for 30 seconds in a safe microwave bowl until they melt.
2. Stir the chocolate and, if not completely melted, boil in the microwave at 10-second intervals and stop stirring between each until it is completely melted.
3. Bake the dark chocolate melted on a baking sheet covered with parchment in a uniform thin layer (1/8 inch thick).
4. Clean the microwave-safe container and heat the chocolate chips with milk in the microwave for 30 seconds or until it melts.
5. Combine peanut butter, stevia drops and salt in melted milk chocolate chips in a combination.
6. Sprinkle the peanut butter mixture over the dark chocolate and use a skewer to shake the layers.
7. Place in the refrigerator until it is firm, about 1 hour. Break into pieces and enjoy.

Chai Hot Chocolate:

Serves: 2
Preparation Time: 19 minutes
<u>Nutritional information per serving:</u>
Calories: 161
Fat: 17.3 g
Net Carbs: 2.5 g
Protein: 2.5 g
<u>Ingredients:</u>
- 2 chai tea bags
- ½ cups hot water, divided
- 4 tablespoons cacao powder
- 1 cup unsweetened almond milk
- ½ teaspoons stevia powder
- 4 tablespoons cacao butter

<u>Instructions for Cooking:</u>
1. Place the tea bags and 2 tablespoons of hot water in a bowl and let it steep for about 5 minutes.
2. In a small pan, add the cacao powder and the remaining water and beat well.
3. Add the almond milk and stir to combine.
4. Stir in the stevia and cacao butter.
5. Discard the tea bags and pour the tea into the pan.
6. Cook for about 2-4 minutes or until butter is dissolved completely, stirring continuously.
7. Remove the pan from heat and transfer into serving cups.
8. Serve immediately.

Creamy Coconut Porridge:

Serves: 2

Preparation Time: 15 minutes

<u>Nutritional information per serving:</u>

Calories: 300

Fat: 25.1 g

Net Carbs: 8 g

Protein: 4.9 g

<u>Ingredients:</u>

- 4 tablespoons coconut flour
- 2 tablespoons flaxseed meal
- 1 tablespoon pumpkin seeds, ground
- 2 tablespoons pecans, ground
- 1/4 teaspoon ground cinnamon
- 1/2 teaspoon vanilla paste
- 1/2 cup canned coconut milk
- 1/2 cup water
- 4 tablespoons double cream
- 4 tablespoons xylitol

<u>Instructions for Cooking:</u>

1. Mix the ingredients in a sauté pan over moderate heat.
2. Now, simmer the mixture for about 8 minutes or until thoroughly heated.
3. Divide your porridge between two serving bowls and serve warm. Devour!

Strawberry Chocolate Mousse:

Serves: 2
Preparation Time: 30 minutes
Nutritional information per serving:
Calories: 567
Fat: 45.6 g
Net Carbs: 9.6 g
Protein: 13.6 g
Ingredients:
- 3 eggs
- ½ cups dark chocolate chips
- 1 cup heavy cream
- 1 cup fresh strawberries, sliced
- 1 vanilla extract
- 1 tablespoon xylitol

Instructions for Cooking:
1. In a bowl, melt the chocolate in the microwave for a minute on high and let it cool for 10 minutes.
2. In another bowl, whip the cream until very soft. Add the eggs, vanilla extract, and xylitol; whisk to combine. Fold in the cooled chocolate.
3. Divide the mousse between glasses, top with the strawberry slices and chill in the fridge for at least 30 minutes before serving.

Golden Flax Seed and Pecan Pudding:

Serves: 2

Preparation Time: 10 minutes

<u>Nutritional information per serving:</u>

Calories: 327

Fat: 32 g

Net Carbs: 6.7 g

Protein: 4.8 g

<u>Ingredients:</u>

- 2/3 cup water
- 1/2 cup canned coconut milk
- 2 tablespoons pecans, ground
- 2 tablespoons coconut flour
- 2 tablespoons golden flaxseeds, ground
- A few drops of liquid Stevia
- A pinch of grated nutmeg

<u>Instructions for Cooking:</u>

1. Place the water and coconut milk in a sauté pan over medium-high heat; bring to a boil.
2. Add in the remaining items. Turn the heat to medium-low and cook, stirring frequently, for 2 minutes or until thoroughly heated.
3. Divide between two serving bowls and let it cool at room temperature.
4. Transfer to your refrigerator and serve well-chilled. Enjoy!

Spiced Mocha:

Serves: 2
Preparation Time: 15 minutes
Nutritional information per serving:
Calories: 161
Fat: 17 g
Net Carbs: 2.7 g
Protein: 1.8 g
Ingredients:

- 1 cup unsweetened coconut milk
- 2 tablespoons Erythritol
- 2 tablespoons cacao powder
- 1 teaspoon organic vanilla extract
- ½ teaspoon ground cinnamon
- ¼ teaspoon ground cardamom
- Pinch of cayenne pepper
- 1½ cups brewed hot coffee
- 1 tablespoon MCT oil
- 3-4 tablespoons whipped cream

Instructions for Cooking:

1. Place the coconut milk, Erythritol, cacao powder, vanilla extract, and spices in a small pan and mix well.
2. Place the pan over medium heat and convey it to a boil.
3. Cook for about 1 minute.
4. Remove from heat and stir in the coffee and MCT oil until well combined.
5. Transfer into 2 mugs and top each with the whipped cream.
6. Serve immediately.

Chocolate and Coconut Fudge Brownies:

Serves: 2

Preparation Time: 25 minutes

Nutritional information per serving:

Calories: 405

Fat: 40 g

Net Carbs: 8.8 g

Protein: 6.3 g

Ingredients:

- 2 tablespoons ground flax
- 1/4 cup coconut flour
- 1/4 teaspoon baking powder
- 1/4 teaspoon cinnamon
- 1/4 teaspoon cardamom
- 2 tablespoons cocoa powder
- 1/3 cup xylitol
- 1 tablespoon dark rum
- 1/4 cup coconut oil
- 1 egg, beaten
- 1-ounce sugar-free dark chocolate, melted
- 1/4 teaspoon coconut extract

Instructions for Cooking:

1. Mix the ground flax, coconut flour, baking powder, cinnamon, cardamom, cocoa powder, and xylitol in a mixing bowl.
2. In another mixing bowl, mix the remaining ingredients until everything is well combined.
3. Add the wet mixture to the dry mixture; mix to combine well. Spoon the batter in a lightly greased baking pan.
4. Bake in the preheated oven at 360₀ F for 18 to 20 minutes or until a tester comes out dry and clean. Bon appétit!